Born in 1941 in Tokyo, **Hayao Miyazaki** is known as the 'Japanese Disney', a filmmaker as revered – and as popular – as Walt Disney or Steven Spielberg. Miyazaki, in short, is a true phenomenon in contemporary animation and in contemporary cinema, a director of animated movies that range from the lyrical, whimsical and child-like beauty of *My Neighbor Totoro* and *Ponyo On the Cliff By the Sea* to the epic sweep of *Nausicaä of the Valley of the Wind* and *Princess Mononoke*.

This book focusses on Miyazaki's 2001 masterpiece ***Spirited Away***, winner of the Best Animated Movie Oscar.

MEDIA, FEMINISM, CULTURAL STUDIES

The Sacred Cinema of Andrei Tarkovsky
by Jeremy Mark Robinson

Liv Tyler
by Thomas A. Christie

Disney Business, Disney Films, Disney Lands
The Wonderful World of the Walt Disney Company
Daniel Cerruti

Steven Spielberg: God-light
by Jeremy Mark Robinson

The Poetry of Cinema
by John Madden

Stepping Forward: Essays, Lectures and Interviews
by Wolfgang Iser

Wild Zones: Pornography, Art and Feminism
by Kelly Ives

Global Media Warning: Explorations of Radio, Television and the Press
by Oliver Whitehorne

'Cosmo Woman': The World of Women's Magazines
by Oliver Whitehorne

The Cinema of Richard Linklater
by Thomas A. Christie

Walerian Borowczyk
by Jeremy Mark Robinson

Andrea Dworkin
by Jeremy Mark Robinson

Cixous, Irigaray, Kristeva: The Jouissance of French Feminism
by Kelly Ives

The Erotic Object: Sexuality in Sculpture
From Prehistory to the Present Day
by Susan Quinnell

Women in Pop Music
by Helen Challis

Detonation Britain: Nuclear War in the UK
by Jeremy Mark Robinson

Julia Kristeva: Art, Love, Melancholy, Philosophy, Semiotics
by Kelly Ives

Luce Irigaray: Lips, Kissing, and the Politics of Sexual Difference
by Kelly Ives

Helene Cixous I Love You: The Jouissance of Writing
by Kelly Ives

Feminism and Shakespeare
by B.D. Barnacle

SPIRITED AWAY

HAYAO MIYAZAKI

POCKET MOVIE GUIDE

JEREMY MARK ROBINSON

SPIRITED AWAY

POCKET MOVIE GUIDE

CRESCENT MOON

First published 2012.
© Jeremy Mark Robinson 2012.

Printed and bound in the U.S.A.
Set in Helvetica Neue Condensed, 9 on 14 point.
Designed by Radiance Graphics.

The right of Jeremy Mark Robinson to be identified as the author of this book has been asserted generally in accordance with sections 77 and 78 of the Copyright, Designs and Patents Act 1988.

All rights reserved. No part of this book may be reprinted or reproduced, stored in a retrieval system, or transmitted, in any form or by any means, electronic, mechanical, photocopying, recording or otherwise, without permission from the publisher.

British Library Cataloguing in Publication data available for this title.

ISBN-13 9781861713476 (Pbk)

Crescent Moon Publishing
P.O. Box 1312, Maidstone, Kent
ME14 5XU, U.K.
www.crmoon.com
cresmopub@yahoo.co.uk

CONTENTS

Acknowledgements   *10*
Abbreviations   *11*
Illustrations   *13*

1   Introduction: The Cinema of Hayao Miyazaki   *17*
2   Hayao Miyazaki's Movies and the Japanese Animation Industry   *35*
3   Aspects of Hayao Miyazaki's Cinema   *60*
     Illustrations   *97*
4   *Spirited Away*   *119*

Resources   *179*
Quotes By Hayao Miyazaki   *181*
Critics On *Spirited Away*   *183*
Filmographies   *185*
Bibliography   *195*

ACKNOWLEDGEMENTS

To the authors and publishers quoted.
Thanks to Peter van der Lugt at GhibliWorld.com.
Thanks to Emily for many conversations about Miyazaki.

PICTURE CREDITS

Illustrations are © Hayao Miyazaki. Studio Ghibli. Nibariki. Toho. Tokuma Shoten. Hakuhodo. Geneon. Buena Vista Home Entertainment Japan. Buena Vista Distribution. Walt Disney Pictures. Optimum Releasing. Tokuma International.

Images are used for information and research purposes, with no infringement of copyright or rights intended.

ABBREVIATIONS

SP Hayao Miyazaki, *Starting Point*
M   Helen McCarthy, *Hayao Miyazaki*
C   Dan Cavallaro, *The Anime Art of Hayao Miyazaki*
O   C. Odell & M. Le Blanc, *Studio Ghibli*

(Images from Spirited Away
© Nibariki/ TGNDDTM, 2001)

#1

INTRODUCTION

THE CINEMA OF HAYAO MIYAZAKI

Born on January 5, 1941 in Tokyo, Hayao Miyazaki[1] is known as the 'Japanese Disney', a filmmaker as revered – and as popular – as Walt Disney or Steven Spielberg. Miyazaki, in short, is a true phenomenon in contemporary animation and in contemporary cinema.

For many people, particularly in the Western world, the first Hayao Miyazaki movie they would have seen would probably be *Princess Mononoke* or *Spirited Away*. Those were the two films that really brought Miyazaki to the attention of a big audience in the West. *Spirited Away* was one of Hayao Miyazaki's and Studio Ghibli's biggest hits: it was the highest grossing movie in Japanese history; it won numerous awards, including the Oscar for Best Animated Feature, and the critics adored it. Three months after its release, *Spirited Away* had sold one ticket for every six people in Japan.

Hayao Miyazaki may be the most talented fantasy filmmaker of his generation: not even the finest filmmakers of Hollywood could rival his films when it came to creating

---
[1] This book on *Spirited Away* uses chapters from my book *The Cinema of Hayao Miyazaki* (Crescent Moon, 2011), which have been revised.

fantasy worlds, and fantastical characters and events.[2]

Once you've seen a Hayao Miyazaki animated movie, you don't forget it. We have seen all of the elements in Miyazaki's films before, it's true, but not brought together in quite this way, and rarely achieved with such skill, such delicacy, such vision.

What Hayao Miyazaki's movies do is to bring you completely into a fantasy world that is instantly recognizable and familiar. It's as if these fantasy realms *have always existed* – very like J.R.R. Tolkien's Middle-earth or Ursula Le Guin's Earthsea (both influences on Miyazaki). The bathhouse in *Spirited Away* is so completely realized, it *must* exist, somewhere (and it does – in a movie – and in the minds of millions of people. And we know that when something lodges itself in the mind, it can be as real and as valuable as anything in the exterior world). The visionary and magical elements are fused with the domestic and familial and social elements, so that it seems completely ordinary and believable that, say, flying machines soar overhead which have flapping wings like an insect (as in *Laputa: Castle In the Sky*), or that little white creatures pop up out of trees (as in *Princess Mononoke*).[3]

In Hayao Miyazaki's fantasy cinema, the immersion in the world is total, and there's nothing to lift you out of it. There are no winks at the camera, no sending up, no intrusive movie allusions or pop culture quotes. The films of Miyazaki and his teams guide you into the filmic world with such confidence and such flair and imagination, you are happy to step inside. Partly it's because, as with the fantasy realms of Tolkien or Le Guin, Miyazaki and his teams are drawing on a long and detailed tradition of fantasy – in literature, mythology and folk tales as well as cinema. It is, in short, partly the realm of fairy tales, the classic fantasy worlds that seem to have always existed. It is that world of 'once upon a time', a place where

---
[2] I agree with Mark Schilling who said that 'none of his contemporaries can equal the richness, depth and strangeness of his imagination' (2004).

[3] One of the hallmarks of *manga* and Japanese entertainment was 'twisting both time and space', Miyazaki said, in order to 'create a more fantastic, magical world' (SP, 99).

people are put under spells, monsters roam the deep forests, and magic crystals can keep castles afloat in the sky.

Hayao Miyazaki really enjoys creating imaginary worlds – that joy in creation bounces off the screen in all of his features and TV work. It's about fashioning lies and fakery so intensely it persuades the audience that it's real, that such a world might really exist.

> It's an imaginary world [Miyazaki explained], but it should seem to actually exist as an alternate world, and the people who live there should appear to think and act in a realistic way. (SP, 307)

It's all lies in animation, Hayao Miyazaki stated in 1979, it's all a fabrication of something that the animators want the audience to believe is real:

> Even if the world depicted is a lie, the trick is to make it seem as real as possible. Stated another way, the animator must fabricate a lie that seems so real viewers will think the world depicted might possibly exist. (SP, 21)

Audiences *want* to believe, of course. They *yearn* to think that some fantasy world can really exist. And they want to go there.

🌾

Spirited Away was released on July 20, 2001 (and on September 20, 2002 in the U.S.A.). The other animated feature films directed by Hayao Miyazaki are (with the Japanese release date first):

🌾 *The Castle of Cagliostro* (1979), released: December 15, 1979. U.S.A. release: Sept, 1980 and April 4, 1991.
🌾 *Nausicaä of the Valley of the Wind* (1984), released: March 11, 1984. U.S.A. release: June, 1985.
🌾 *Laputa: Castle In the Sky* (1986), released: August 2, 1986. U.S.A. release: July, 1987 and April 1, 1989.
🌾 *My Neighbor Totoro* (1988), released: April 16, 1988.

U.S.A. release: May 7, 1993.
* *Kiki's Delivery Service* (1989), released: July 29, 1989. U.S.A. release: May 23, 1998 (video).
* *Porco Rosso* (1992), released: July 20, 1992. U.S.A. release: October 9, 2003.
* *Princess Mononoke* (1997), released: July 12, 1997. U.S.A. release: October 7, 1999.
* *Howl's Moving Castle* (2004), released: November 20, 2004. U.S.A. release: June 6, 2005.
* *Ponyo On the Cliff By the Sea* (2008), released: July 19, 2008. U.S.A. release: June 28, 2009.

These are some of the most remarkable, inventive and entertaining movies in the history of cinema.

Spirited Away was an original script by Hayao Miyazaki (his other scripts have included *Laputa: Castle In the Sky, Nausicaä of the Valley of the Wind, Porco Rosso, My Neighbor Totoro, Ponyo On the Cliff By the Sea* and *Princess Mononoke*. That's two-thirds of Miyazaki's feature movie output: the other films have been based on books or *manga* – *Kiki's Delivery Service, Howl's Moving Castle,* and of course *The Castle of Cagliostro*.

To write one hit animation movie is amazing, to write *ten* is remarkable. To write *and* direct one spectacular animated picture is very impressive, to *write and direct ten features* is unheard-of in the world of contemporary commercial animation. There's no one in Hollywood or the West with a similar track record. (In the West, for instance, including Hollywood cinema, such as from Disney, Pixar, Warners, DreamWorks, Fox, etc, it's typical for animated movies to have whole teams of writers and story artists). So Hayao Miyazaki really is a one-of-a-kind filmmaker. (And Miyazaki has said that he hasn't seen *any* of the recent animated movies of the West, including the celebrated products of Pixar).

Whatever the literary (or *manga*) source, however, all of Hayao Miyazaki's films bear a strong imprint from the director himself. It's true that animation, like all filmmaking, is a very collaborative process,4 and it requires a large team years of hard work to complete one of these feature animated movies. But it's also true that Miyazaki is one of the very, very few film directors working in the animation industry who can truly, properly and authentically be called an *auteur*, an artist who has a major influence on his films.

But how many true *auteurs* in feature animation (not shorts) of recent times are there? Jan Svankmajer, certainly; Walerian Borowczyk, certainly; the Quay brothers, certainly; Henry Selick, perhaps. And then... who?

The form of Hayao Miyazaki's animation is cel animation, also known as ink and paint animation, or 2-D animation. It is a traditional form of animated film which is based on drawings and paintings. It is all done by hand, too, with each cel drawn and then painted by hand. The process moves from conceptual sketches to storyboards, to key animation and final drawings.

There are so many vital talents in making a feature-length animated film, so this is not to underplay the roles of Hayao Miyazaki's producer, Toshio Suzuki, his co-producer at Studio Ghibli, Isao Takahata, or animators such as Kitaro Kousaka, Masashi Ando, Kazuo Komatsubara, Tsukasa Tannai, Akihiro Yamashita, Takeshi Inaumura and Megumi Kagawa; editor Takeshi Seyama, or composer Joe Hisaishi, or colour designer Michiyo Yasuda, or sound people Toru Noguchi, Shuji Inoue, Kazuhiro Hayashi, Kazuhiro Wakabayashi, and Nobue Yoshinaga. Most of these folk worked on *Spirited Away*.

Spirited Away was produced nearly entirely at Studio Ghibli, an animation studio best known for the fantasy films of Hayao Miyazaki, but it also produced other pictures, as well as TV shows, TV specials and commercial work. The other main film director at Ghibli was Isao Takahata, who directed *Grave of the Fireflies* (1988), *Only Yesterday* (1991), *Pon Poko*

---

4 Hayao Miyazaki recognized that directors and writers could be over-emphasized in the creation of an animated work. Animation was a team effort, and no element should be over-emphasized while others were ignored (SP, 64). And sometimes there was too much attention given to the original work.

(*Defenders of the Forest,* 1994), and *My Neighbors the Yamadas* (1999).

HAYAO MIYAZAKI'S BIOGRAPHY AND CAREER

Hayao Miyazaki grew up during World War Two in Japan, and was evacuated from Tokyo in 1944; he started school in 1947, still away from the capital (the Miyazaki family moved back to Tokyo in 1950). At Gakushuin University, Miyazaki studied political science and economics. Politics has always played a significant role in Miyazaki's career. Miyazaki was active in the union at Toei Animation, for example, becoming the Chief Secretary in 1964; at Toei he was involved in a labour dispute in 1964.

The Miyazaki family business was – no surprise here – an aviation company. Hayao Miyazaki's father, Katsuji Miyazaki (1915-93), was one of the directors of the company, which constructed parts for Japanese Zero fighter planes during World War 2.[5]

Hayao Miyazaki married a fellow animator, Akemi Ota, in 1965; their children include Goro Miyazaki (b. 1967), who later turned to directing. It was also around this time that Miyazaki met and grew friends with Isao Takahata; Ota and Takahata are perhaps the key collaborators of Miyazaki's career. Wives, husbands or lovers are often overlooked by film critics when discussing the influences on a filmmaker's life, but it's safe to assume that Akemi Ota would have had a considerable influence on Miyazaki's cinema – not least because she is an animator herself.

After he left university in 1963, Hayao Miyazaki joined the

---

[5] Hayao Miyazaki's father worked at the Miyazaki Airplane Corporation, in Kanuma City, which was owned by his uncle, Miyazaki said, making parts for war planes (not all of the parts worked, either [SP, 208]). Certainly there's an ambiguity about Miyazaki's attitude towards what his father did for a living, in manufacturing machines that were used for war. That plays against Miyazaki's fascination for wars (C, 7).

Toei Animation company, where he began working in the in-between department, on TV shows such as *Wolf Boy Ken* (1963) and *Watchdog Woof-Woof* (1963). Miyazaki moved into key animation at Toei, contributing to the TV series *Wind Ninja Boy Fujimaru* (1964). Miyazaki also worked on *Hustle Punch* (1965), and *Rainbow Warrior Robin* (1966).

Other credits of Hayao Miyazaki's include the feature film *The Little Norse Prince* (1968), which was directed by Isao Takahata, the TV series *Little Witch Sally* (1968), *Akko-chan's Secret* (1969), the feature film *Puss In Boots* (1969), *The Impudent Frog* (1971), *Sarutobi Etchan* (1971), and the features *The Flying Ghost Ship* (1969), *Animal Treasure Island* (1971), and *Ali Baba and the 40 Thieves* (1971).

In 1971, Hayao Miyazaki and Isao Takahata left Toei to join A-Pro. They went on to work for Zuiyo Company, and Nippon Animation. Miyazaki's first film as director, 1979's *The Castle of Cagliostro,* was produced by Tokyo Movie Shinsha. Miyazaki also directed some of the TV episodes of the *Lupin III* series (in 1971) with his colleague Takahata. (This show ran for 23 episodes, and Miyazaki and Takahata worked on 17 episodes as directors).

In the 1970s, Hayao Miyazaki was working in television animation, the backbone of the Japanese animation industry: *Akado Suzunosuke* (1972), *Wilderness Boy Isamu* (1973), *Samurai Giants* (1973), *Alpine Girl Heidi* (1974), *A Dog of Flanders* (1975), *Three Thousand Miles In Search of Mother* (1976), *Rascal the Raccoon* (1977), *Future Boy Conan* (1978) and *Anne of Green Gables* (1979).

For some of these TV animated series, Isao Takahata was directing, with Hayao Miyazaki providing concepts, scripts, layouts and key animation:[6] *Three Thousand Miles In Search of Mother*, *Alpine Girl Heidi* and *Anne of Green Gables*. Three

---

[6] Both Takahata and Miyazaki have discussed the issue of whether Miyazaki might've made more movies if he hadn't met Takahata or hadn't worked for Takahata. Miyazaki thought the idea was silly, and he had been quite happy being an animator: 'I had no complaint about being an animator. If I thought about my work at such a level as expressing myself in such a form, or self-display, or showing my personality, I think I could have only done a worse job'.

Thousand Miles In Search of Mother was based on Edmondo de Amici's *Cuore* (1886). *Anne of Green Gables* derived from the novels of Lucy Maude Montgomery (early 1900s). *Rascal Raccoon* (1977) was part of Nippon Animation's *World Masterpiece Theater* TV series, and was based on Sterling North's writings about his childhood in Wisconsin. Miyazaki worked as a key animator on it (and chiefly as a scenic designer on the other shows).

Alpine Girl Heidi was an important work for both Takahata and Miyazaki, not least because it was successful with audiences and broadcasters. The success led to a feature movie being released, culled, as so often with television *animé*, from the TV episodes re-worked into a feature-length piece. *Heidi* was based on the fiction of Johanna Spyri, and included images of life in the mountains which would influence Miyazaki's later films.

Miyazaki and Takahata collaborated on some short films about the adventures of a panda and his chums, with Takahata directing from designs and a script by Miyazaki: *Panda Go Panda* (*Panda & Child,* 1973), and *The Adventures of Panda and Friends* (1972).[7]

Panda Go Panda is fun, colourful, light-hearted; the comedy is typical of Isao Takahata's work. For Hayao Miyazaki fans *Panda Go Panda* looks forward to themes, images and motifs that crop up in later outings. Such as visuals like Mimiko's hair (Dola in *Laputa: Castle In the Sky* has the same wild plaits), or Daddy Panda's wide grin and portly figure, which leads onto the giant Totoro.

More important for future Hayao Miyazaki movies, however, are the thematic and narrative elements in *Panda Go Panda*, such as Mimi being essentially an orphan (her grandmother leaves her for a week). It's a recurring theme in Miyazaki's cinema – that young children can survive on their own – it crops up in *Laputa: Castle In the Sky,* for instance, with both Pazu and Sheeta, or Kiki in *Kiki's Delivery Service,*

---
[7] *Panda Go Panda* has been re-issued on DVD and video.

and right up to *Ponyo On the Cliff By the Sea*, where two five year-old children are left on their own. That is a fundamental ingredient of children's literature, though: authors have to find a way of separating the children from the parents. *Spirited Away* comes up with a very dramatic solution.

In 1978 Hayao Miyazaki directed *Future Boy Conan* (a.k.a. *Conan, the Boy In the Future*) for Nippon Animation, one of his important works, and his first TV series as director (Isao Takahata and Keiji Hayakawa were co-directors, and Yasuo Otsuka was animation director). It comprised 26 episodes of 25 minutes each, with a TV movie edited from the series, entitled *Future Boy Conan: The Movie*. *Future Boy Conan* was based on *The Incredible Tide* (1970) by Alexander Key.[8]

In 1981 Hayao Miyazaki directed the TV series *Great Detective Holmes* (a.k.a. *Sherlock Hound the Detective*), made as a co-production with R.A.I. TV in Italy. It featured Sherlock Holmes-style capers in a dog world (a world populated only by dog characters). On *Great Detective Holmes* Miyazaki worked with Italian animators, including his friend Marco Pagott (he later named the character of Porco Rosso after Pagott).

Television animation continued into the 1980s and beyond for Hayao Miyazaki, although from *Nausicaä of the Valley of the Wind* onwards much of Miyazaki's work in animation was confined to his own movies: Miyazaki did key animation in *New Adventures of Gigantor* (1980), directed two episodes of *Lupin III* (1980), directed the first six episodes of *Great Detective Holmes* (1981),[9] and contributed key animation to the film *Space Adventure Cobra* (1982) and the TV show *Zorro* (1982).

Hayao Miyazaki formed his own company, Nibariki (Two-Horse Power) in 1984, and Studio Ghibli a little later,[10] with Isao Takahata, Toshio Suzuki and Toru Hara (former president

---
[8] In 1999 the series was revived as *Future Boy Conan: Taiga Adventure* (directed by Keiji Hayakawa, Miyazaki's former assistant).
[9] There was a short film released in cinemas.
[10] The first Studio Ghibli film officially was *Laputa: Castle In the Sky*, but *Nausicaä of the Valley of the Wind* (1984) was really the first Studio Ghibli production (although it had been produced at Topcraft).

of Topcraft). The first Ghibli studio was in Kichijoji in Tokyo, the second in Koganei.[11] In 1995 Miyazaki and Ghibli made a pop music video for the band Chage and Aska.

The *manga* work of Hayao Miyazaki shouldn't be overlooked: it has provided the basis for feature films such as *Porco Rosso* and *Nausicaä of the Valley of the Wind* and has influenced movies that Miyazaki didn't direct, such as *Tales From Earthsea*.

Hayao Miyazaki's *manga* includes a history of food on airlines (*Dining In the Air*); *Puss In Boots* (1969); *People of the Desert* (1972), a war piece; *Animal Treasure Island* (1982); *To My Sister* (1983); *The Journey of Shuna* (1983); *Daydream Data Notes* (1984-92), a World War Two story about a German tank commander; *Miscellaneous Notes: The Age of Seaplanes* (1989), which led towards *Porco Rosso*; the World War 2 story *The Return of Hans* (1994); and *Tiger In the Mire* (1998). Miyazaki and Studio Ghibli have also produced '*Art of*' books for each Ghibli movie, which are useful sources of information.

STUDIO GHIBLI

Studio Ghibli is an in-house animation production company: by the early 1990s and its move to its new premises in West Tokyo, it had the staff and resources to produce everything except the sound in an animated movie. It has the staff to create a movie from scratch, including the photography and computer generated work (two computer-controlled cameras were used to photograph animation). Studio Ghibli has edited its movies digitally (on an Avid system) since 1998 (in common with the commercial movie industry in general).

The Studio Ghibli feature films are:

---

[11] The animation under the Topcraft ægis had been produced at Asagaya in the Suhinami ward in Tokyo (SP, 443).

Nausicaä of the Valley of the Wind (produced at Topcraft, but essentially a Ghibli film)
Laputa: Castle In the Sky
My Neighbor Totoro
Grave of the Fireflies
Kiki's Delivery Service
Only Yesterday
Porco Rosso
Pon Poko
Whisper of the Heart
Princess Mononoke
My Neighbors the Yamadas
Spirited Away
The Cat Returns
Howl's Moving Castle
Tales From Earthsea
Ponyo On the Cliff By the Sea
The Borrower Arriety
From Up On Poppy Hill

Best known for their movies, Studio Ghibli also produces work for advertising and television (like all Hollywood studios, and most animation studios). Movies might be what the animation studios are known for, but they have to pay the bills, and commercial work is vital (for Ghibli, merchandizing also plays a key role, bringing in revenue during leaner years between the big hit movies like *Spirited Away* or *Princess Mononoke*).[12] Ghibli produced some TV idents for NTV in 1992 (*Sky-Coloured Seed*), and 5 TV commercials (in 2001), plus others.

The big earner, as far as licensed characters are con-

---

[12] Producer Toshio Suzuki has said that he would prefer it if a movie could make all its money back from a theatrical release, without needing video or DVD sales, let alone merchandizing (M, 207). However, in the global marketplace, sales to home entertainment formats like DVD and video can't be ignored: a Hollywood picture, for instance, will typically take less than a quarter of its total revenue from being shown in theatres. Of course, with Hayao Miyazaki's movies being such hits, they could make their money back from theatrical release alone.

cerned, is Totoro, derived from *My Neighbor Totoro*. Totoro as a character and image, a mascot – like the film itself – is tailor-made for merchandizing. And it is Totoro, of course, who was chosen as the Studio Ghibli company logo (it's a drawing of Totoro against a mid-blue background).[13]

Studio Ghibli is among the most successful animation houses in Japan in recent times: although it is one studio among hundreds in Japan, it absorbs a high proportion of ticket sales at the theatre or video and DVD sales, or television viewing figures (35.1% of the audience watched *Princess Mononoke* when it was broadcast on TV in Japan in 1999).[14] This's largely due to the movies directed by Miyazaki.

Prior to *Princess Mononoke*, Hayao Miyazaki and his team at Studio Ghibli had had big hits and number one films, but *Princess Mononoke* went through the roof. It was the highest grossing movie[15] in Japanese history (unadjusted for inflation), until *Spirited Away*. In 1997, only *Titanic* (that one-off phenomenon that no one can fully explain – or replicate) beat it at the box office.

In 1996, the Walt Disney corporation brokered a deal with the Japanese animation studio to distribute its films in the U.S.A. and Canada. Disney set about Americanizing the movies by dubbing them into American English, sometimes using well-known actors (like Michael Keaton and Carey Elwes in *Porco Rosso*, or Claire Danes, Gillian Anderson, Billy Crudup, and Keith David in *Mononoke Hime*). John Lasseter, later head honcho of Pixar, acknowledged the influence of Miyazaki's films. Crucially, it meant that Studio Ghibli's

---

13 Isao Takahata praised Hayao Miyazaki for creating such an endearing mascot in Totoro – Totoros were now found throughout Japan, Takahata said: 'Totoro lives in the hearts of all children throughout Japan, and when they see trees now, they sense Totoro hidden in them. And this is a truly wonderful and indeed rare thing' (2009, 457).

14 Mamoru Oshii commented: 'What do other animators think of Ghibli? As far as I know, they basically respect Ghibli. It's half love, and half hate. A general response would be: it's a tremendous place, but I don't want to go there. Because they control you too tightly (at Ghibli).'

15 Once again, one should remember that it's box office *rentals* not box office *gross* that is the more accurate indicator of a film's financial returns. And figures should always be *adjusted for inflation*, otherwise they're even more inaccurate.

movies had a much wider release (in the West), and many more people got to see them.

INFLUENCES

Hayao Miyazaki has remarked that his influences are probably innumerable. At university, Miyazaki encountered some of the classic authors of children's fiction, including Eleanor Farjeon, Phillipa Pearce, and Rosemary Sutcliffe (he joined the children's literature group). Ryotaro Shiba, Yoshie Hotaa, and Sasuke Nakao were also influences.

Treasure Island (1883) by Robert Louis Stevenson is a key literary influence on Hayao Miyazaki, and Jules Verne, of course, Mark Twain, Jonathan Swift, Maurice Leblanc, and Antoine de Saint-Exupéry. Among science fiction and fantasy authors, Miyazaki has cited Brian Aldiss (*Hothouse*), Frank Herbert (*Dune*), Isaac Asimov (*Nightfall*), J.R.R. Tolkien (*The Lord of the Rings*), Diana Wynne-Jones, and Ursula Le Guin (particularly her *Earthsea* series). He told Le Guin when he visited her that he kept her books by his bed, and had been re-reading her works for years.

Among filmmakers, Hayao Miyazaki has often cited the Russian film *The Snow Queen* (Lev Atamatov, 1957) as an important influence. Miyazaki wrote fondly of *The Tale of the White Serpent*. Both *The Snow Queen* and *The Tale of the White Serpent* were important influences for the young Miyazaki. But he was later critical of both movies, perhaps embarrassed by loving them so much as a kid.

Among the animation influences on the young Hayao Miyazaki were toons such as Mickey Mouse and Betty Boop.[16] Much of the time animated films were scarce when Miyazaki went to the movies: he said maybe they would see one Disney

---

[16] Miyazaki has cited the Fleischers as an influence. In 1980, while discussing the Fleischers in *FILM*, he noted that the endings of the Fleischers' cartoons were poor (SP, 118).

Donald Duck or *Mickey Mouse* short during a Summer (SP, 123). Miyazaki has also mentioned animation coming out of Nihon Dogasha and Toei Animation, as well as the *manga* of Sanpei Shirato (SP, 194).

A big influence on Hayao Miyazaki's early development as an artist was the comicbook artist Osamu Tezuka (1928-89). 'I've been powerfully influenced by Tezuka', Miyazaki admitted, and began to draw *manga* under Tezuka's shadow (SP, 193). Miyazaki recalled that he consciously tried to move away from being 'heavily influenced' by Tezuka's comics and characters. Miyazaki has stated that 'Tezuka's influences buried deep within me proved an extremely heavy burden'.[17]

Osamu Tezuka is of course one of the major figures in Japanese *animé*, creator/ director of *Astro Boy, Arabian Nights, Princess Knight, Triton of the Sea, Kimba the White Lion, Bix X, Black Jack, Dororo, Jungle Emperor Leo*, and *Phoenix*.[18]

Yasuo Otsuka (b. 1931) was a key influence on Hayao Miyazaki. Miyazaki spoke fondly of his co-worker Otsuka, and how he encouraged Miyazaki in many ways, including to see the fun in making animation, and to select material and co-workers carefully (SP, 192). And Miyazaki admitted that sometimes he pushed Otsuka hard, too: when he was directing *The Castle of Cagliostro*, Miyazaki said, Otsuka 'worked hard on *Cagliostro*. He never left his desk. It may have been because I didn't let him' (SP, 331). Otsuka had worked on the first *Lupin* TV series.

---

17 And Tezuka was in turn heavily influenced by Disney: he saw *Bambi* 80 times!
18 As well as 21 TV series and twelve TV specials, Tezuka also produced 700 stories and around 17,000 *manga* pages (C, 30).

FANS OF MIYAZAKI.

In North America, Hayao Miyazaki's movies have some dedicated fans, not least animators at Pixar and Disney,[19] who have often cited Miyazaki's movies as an inspiration. But that hasn't translated into big sales theatrically. For instance, when *Howl's Moving Castle* was released on 202 screens in the U.S.A. in 2005, it grossed only $4.7 million (compared to $190m in Japan). As the box office figures are so high in Japan, Studio Ghibli's and Miyazaki's films can easily sustain themselves without needing overseas sales. But it's a pity, because Miyazaki's movies would appeal to a large American audience, if they came to see them.

The influence of Japanese animation on Western movie-making is *enormous* – in terms of style, action, characters, settings, stories, and everything else. You can see it in the newer *Star Wars* trilogy, in *Avatar*,[20] the *Matrix* films, the *Lord of the Rings* movies, *A.I.*, the *Batman* pictures (and any super-hero movie).

John Lasseter spoke about Hayao Miyazaki's films:

> From a pure filmmaking standpoint, his staging, his cutting, his action scenes are some of the best ever put on film, whether animated or not... Watching one of his films is the best medicine when you have writer's block. When we at Pixar feel that we're beating our heads against the wall, we go in the screening room and put on a laser disc and watch one of his films and it's like, whoa look what he did.[21]

---

[19] Films such as Disney's *Atlantis* directly took up some of Hayao Miyazaki's concepts and visuals – not least the early 20th century setting, with its world of bolts and steel and steam-powered machines. The combination in *Atlantis* of the secret world, the adventure journey to reach it, the technology employed to get there, the flying machines, the gang of characters, and the spiritual under-pinnings, all of these could be found in Miyazaki's cinema. Another one was *Steam-boy*, Katsuhiro Otomo's adventure tale entirely centred around steam and machinery.

[20] Many viewers noted the influence of the floating islands in *Laputa: Castle In the Sky* on *Avatar* (2009).

[21] Quoted in R. Lyman, "Darkly Mythic World Arrives From Japan", *New York Times*, Oct 21, 1999.

Other admirers of Hayao Miyazaki include Barry Cook and Tony Bancroft, Gary Trousdale and Kirk Wise, animator Glen Keane, director Hendel Butoy, director Kevin Altieri, and director Katsuhiro Otomo. Among critics: Andrew Osmond, Roger Ebert, Helen McCarthy, Dan Cavallaro and Jonathan Clements.

Aside from many of the key artists at Disney and Pixar, noted above, fans of Hayao Miyazaki's cinema include Tsui Hark (perhaps the greatest action filmmaker in the world), Guillemo del Toro and Akira Kurosawa: the *sensei* loved *My Neighbor Totoro* and *Kiki's Delivery Service*:

> It's *animé*, but I was so moved. I really loved Nekobus. You wouldn't come up with such an idea. I cried when I watched *Kiki's Delivery Service*.

UNMADE FILMS.

A filmmaker such as Hayao Miyazaki is bursting with ideas, and over the course of his film career, like every major filmmaker, he will have produced many ideas and scripts and drawings and even filmed animation that never quite made it into a finished form or released product. There were some projects that Miyazaki began work on, but left, sometimes due to 'creative differences' between the project's producers and the director. Some projects Miyazaki wouldn't have been able to find funding for. Part of the reason for this is that Miyazaki is a perfectionist, workaholic kind of filmmaker, and those sorts of projects take a lot of work and a lot of time (and a lot of money) to complete.

In 2006 Hayao Miyazaki said he wanted to make a movie about Edo Castle and the 15th century period. Another unrealized project was about the survivors of the Great Kanto Earthquake of 1923. Prior to *Spirited Away* the project *Rin the Chimney Painter* had been developed but cancelled (Miyazaki wanted to set it at the time of the 1923 quake).

ISAO TAKAHATA.

Isao Takahata (born October 29, 1935, in Ise, Japan), known to his colleagues and friends as Paku-san, is one of the most important people in Hayao Miyazaki's artistic career: they produced each other's work while the other was directing. As Miyazaki has acknowledged, they often clashed when working together, and had learnt to be very 'hands off' when they were producing the other's projects. According to the 'making of' documentary of *Only Yesterday*, while working on the movie, Miyazaki said they rarely talked – and Miyazaki was producing the film! After a screening of the finished picture, Miyazaki walked out without saying anything.

Isao Takahata is the other main director at Studio Ghibli, and has directed films such as *Ponpoko, Panda! Go Panda!, 3000 Leagues In Search of Mother, My Neighbors the Yamadas, Gauche the Cellist, Only Yesterday* and *Grave of the Fireflies*. Also, Takahata had directing credits long before Miyazaki, helming TV shows such as *Apache Baseball Team, Heidi, 3000 Leagues In Search of Mother* and *Anne of Green Gables*. Takahata's first feature film as director was 1968's *The Little Norse Prince* (a.k.a. *Horusu: Prince of the Sun*). The financial failure of that movie led to Takahata and Miyazaki leaving Toei Animation.

Isao Takahata is a fabulously talented filmmaker, especially good at comedy and broad slapstick. But his films also have an emotional depth which's really striking, and some of them, such as *Only Yesterday* (*Omoide Poro Poro*, 1991), and *Grave of the Fireflies* (*Hotaru no Haka*, 1988), are deeply moving, with *Grave of the Fireflies* delivering an emotional punch that very few (animated) movies have achieved. It's on the scale of distressing emotion of *Bambi*. Indeed, *Grave of the Fireflies* is a masterpiece of cinema, the equal of *anything else* in animation – or live-action.

TOSHIO SUZUKI.

Toshio Suzuki (born 1948), the producer of *Spirited Away*, joined the Studio Ghibli team after meeting Hayao Miyazaki when he was managing editor of *Animage* magazine (founded in 1978), which published Miyazaki's *manga* of *Nausicaä of the Valley of the Wind*. As one of the key players at Studio Ghibli, Suzuki is thus one of the leading figures in the Japanese animation industry, as well as being a vital influence on Miyazaki's cinema. Isao Takahata remarked that without 'Suzuki-san, there would be no Studio Ghibli today', and that Suzuki has 'steadfastly supported Hayao Miyazaki' (2009, 460).

Other key collaborators on Hayao Miyazaki's movies include: Masashi Andou, key animator, Hideaki Anno, key animator (and co-founder of animation studio Gainax), Yoshifumi Kondo, key animator, Mamoru Hosoda (director of two *Digimon* movies), Tomomi Mochizuki, director, Hiroyuki Morita, key animator, Yasuo Otsuka, animation director, Yasuyoshi Tokuma, president of Tokuma Shoten, and Michiyo Yasuda, colour designer and head of the ink and paint dept at Ghibli.

#2

HAYAO MIYAZAKI'S MOVIES AND THE JAPANESE ANIMATION INDUSTRY

Japan has the biggest animation industry in the world, so Hayao Miyazaki's films and those of Studio Ghibli are very much a part of it. That Japan is one of the richest nations on Earth plays a part (at the height of the Bubble Economy in the 1980s, Japan had 16% of the global economic power, and 60% of real estate wealth). The famous TV shows, OAVs, specials, videos, and movies in *animé* include: *Akira, Digimon, Pokémon,*[22] *Dr Slump, Star Blazers, Legend of the Overfiend, Evangelion, Cowboy Bebop, Astro Boy* and *Ghost In the Shell*. According to Helen McCarthy, animation in Japan accounted for 6% of films released in late 1998, 25-30% of videos, and 3-6% of television shows made in Japan. This book isn't an exploration of Japanese *animé*, or the links between the films of Miyazaki and *animé*. There are excellent books on Japanese *animé* available, but I will note a few aspects which throw light on Miyazaki's work.[23]

But Hayao Miyazaki's cinema certainly has numerous links to the Japanese *animé* tradition. For instance, the *shojo* figure (such as Chihiro in *Spirited Away*), the ambiguous

---
[22] The *Pokémon* movies have proved hugely popular in Japan, and rival Studio Ghibli's movies at the box office.
[23] A good place to start, and an essential reference work, is: J. Clements & H. McCarthy's *The Animé Encyclopedia* (Stone Bridge Press, Berkeley, CA, 2001).

treatment of technology, Tokyo settings, Japanese mythology, war (and the two World Wars), the atomic bomb, and the military machine. And the motifs that crop up in thousands of *animé* products are also found in Miyazaki's films: the giant robots, flying, rapid action scenes, explosions, gadgets, steam-punk paraphernalia, young heroes, etc.

At the same time, there are many staples of Japanese *animé* that *don't* appear in Hayao Miyazaki's cinema: high school and classroom scenes, kids riding in cars or on motorcycles, teenage parties, bust-ups between kids and parents, sword fights, and sex (Miyazaki's films steer clear of pornography or even nudity, which form a substantial proportion of Japanese *animé*).

THE JAPANESE *ANIMÉ* INDUSTRY

An important thing to remember about Japanese *animé* is that it is an industry that can sustain itself by producing movies and TV shows for a *domestic audience*: it doesn't need television syndication or releases overseas (but it will always take them up if available). In other words, one of the reasons that the Japanese animation industry is the biggest in the world is because there is such a large market in Japan itself for animation.

That also means that Japanese *animé* filmmakers can make their film and TV shows for a homegrown market, and don't need to pander to an international (or an American) audience. This certainly applies to Hayao Miyazaki's movies, which producer Toshio Suzuki has remarked on a number of occasions are very much *Japanese* movies, movies that are made primarily for the *Japanese* market. So the films can reflect and explore local or national culture, and don't need to build in elements that will appeal to a global audience (no need to shift the action of their films to, say, New York or

Chicago, and turn their characters into Americans).

It's an envious position to be in for a filmmaker. European filmmakers, for instance, can similarly make films only for their own national audience, but they tend to be much smaller (or cheaper) movies. A country such as France can sustain a huge production of movies per year because it has the largest film industry in Europe (that's one of the reasons why French movies travel outside France). And it means that France can make much bigger movies (it has more government investment than many other countries).[24]

Lonely Planet's travel guide to Japan makes some useful points about contemporary Japan:

> First, Japan is an island nation. Second, until WWII, Japan was never conquered by an outside power, nor was it heavily influenced by Christian missionaries. Third, until the beginning of last century, the majority of Japanese lived in close-knit rural farming communities. Fourth, most of Japan is covered in steep mountains, so the few flat areas of the country are quite crowded – people literally live on top of each other. Finally, for almost all of its history, Japan has been a strictly hierarchical place, with something approximating a caste system during the Edo period. (C. Rowthorn, 2007)

As to genres, Hayao Miyazaki's cinema has included many of the chief genres of *animé*, including action-adventure and epics (*Nausicaä of the Valley of the Wind* and *Laputa: Castle In the Sky*), war stories and fantasy (*Howl's Moving Castle*), and Japanese folklore (*Spirited Away* and *Princess Mononoke*). And many of Miyazaki's movies come under the umbrella of 'children's stories'. There is plenty of comedy, though no Miyazaki movie is an out-and-out comedy. Some of Miyazaki's films combine genres: *Porco Rosso*, for example, has elements of romance, comedy, war/ politics, and plenty of

---

[24] And the French love Hayao Miyazaki's movies, as they love comicbooks and fantasy art. One reason that the movies of Miyazaki and Takahata were received better and were more well-known in Europe was because Europe had imported titles such as *Heidi* and *Marco*.

action-adventure.

The genres of Japanese animation include pretty much all of those in live-action, as well some genres particular to *animé*: comedy; romance; crime; action-adventure; horror; historical drama; science fiction (including mecha, cyberpunk, war, epics); fantasy (including comicbooks; supernatural tales; myths and legends; and superheroes); animal stories; martial arts; children's stories; epics; erotica; porn; and sports stories.[25]

In live-action, genres are divided into *jidai-geki*, period movies (typically in the feudal age), and *gendai-geki*, set in the contemporary era.[26] There are further categories within the two genres. Fantasy is one of the key genres of Hayao Miyazaki's cinema, as well as the youth picture.

The Japanese film industry has been one of the most prolific historically, producing over 400 movies a year. The Japanese movie business has been dominated by studio conglomerates, just like the American system, since the 1920s (the biggies are Nikkatsu, Shochiku, Toho,[27] Toei, Shintoho and Daiei). Although the independent film sector has grown since the 1980s, the major studios continue to take up most of film production. And most Japanese film directors work for the major studios in some form or another, or for television.

In Japan, the director is king of the movie-making industry, rather than the star or producer; the director will often appear above the title, and is often used in marketing more than stars. The director is 'the paternalistic head of his own production "family"', as Gerald Mast and Bruce Kawin explain, a social structure which echoes Japanese society (1992b, 409).

Japan is one of the major film markets in the world – for

---

[25] Although it is regarded as popular culture, Japanese *animé* draws on high culture, including woodblock prints, *ukiye-o*, Kabuki theatre, painting, and classical music.
[26] See G. Mast, 1992b, 410.
[27] Toho, founded in the 1930s from a number of smaller companies, is best known as the studio of *Godzilla* and Akira Kurosawa. Miyazaki's later movies have been distributed by Toho.

American movies, yes, but also for movies from everywhere. And when it comes to animation, there is a huge appetite for it in Japan. That helps to sustain an operation like Studio Ghibli, and a filmmaker like Hayao Miyazaki. Without that large, national market, and that enthusiastic response to animated movies and television, it would be more difficult for Miyazaki to make the kind of pictures he wants to make. For instance, if Miyazaki had to use foreign money, the economics would have an impact on the films: an investor from, say, Germany, might have certain requirements about the films being able to play in Europe and the U.S.A. A bank from, say, Australia, might have different provisos.

You can see this operating in blockbuster American movies, which consciously target a range of audiences (casting actors from different countries, for instance). Those ultra-high budget American movies have to make about half their money back from international sales (since the Nineties), so the films have to be able to play in Italy or Egypt or Argentina as well as in America.

But Hayao Miyazaki's films have enjoyed a buoyant market in Japan for home-made animation: in short, the Japanese *animé* industry has enabled Miyazaki's cinema to flourish. In 2006, the best-selling *animé* titles in the U.S. of A. had 6 Studio Ghibli movies in the top 20, and 4 Miyazaki flicks in the top 11 (according to VIZ Media).

Japanese *animé* sells in the Western world via OVAs, videos and DVDs, TV shows, and related *manga* comicbooks. Animated series and movies are prepared for the Western market with English language dubs (nearly always using American actors and American-style English).

Hayao Miyazaki often discussed *manga*, and how it related to Japanese culture and entertainment. *Manga* were certainly huge in Japan, and more so than in any other country (though it was on the increase in some places). America, Miyazaki mused, doesn't have a comicbook tradition anything like *manga* culture in Japan: in Japan, a *manga* like

Shonen Jump might sell 6 million copies a week, enormous numbers. In a 1994 speech, Miyazaki compared that 6 million with the video sales of *Beauty and the Beast* in the U.S.A.: 20 million, for a nation with twice the population of Japan. Selling 20 million in America would be like selling 10 million in Japan, Miyazaki suggested, and *Shonen Jump* sells 6 million *manga* a week!

Certainly *manga* and *animé* have been important in depicting Japanese culture overseas – and it will be for many their first encounter with Japanese culture.[28] According to VIZ Media, the *manga* market in Japan in 2006 was worth $4.28 billion (and $250m in the U.S.A.). *Manga* accounted for around 40% of Japan's printed matter.

The crossover between *manga* and *animé* is well-known (many animations are *manga* first, and *manga* are in turn produced from movies, including Hayao Miyazaki's movies). There is also a crossover into computer games, board games, card games, pop music and online gaming.

CREATING ANIMATION

> Those who join in the work of animation are people who dream more than others and who wish to convey those dreams to others. After a while they realize how incredibly difficult it is to entertain others.
>
> Hayao Miyazaki (SP, 25)

Hayao Miyazaki is a hands-on animation director, a workaholic who oversees every aspect of the animation process. This is unusual: many animation directors oversee projects in detail, but not to the extent of checking every piece of key animation, for instance. Miyazaki has been known to re-draw animation if he thinks it's not good enough. Miyazaki is clearly a filmmaker

---
[28] See G. Poitras, 2001, 8.

who can't resist getting in there and doing the work. He is a filmmaker who really likes to make films.

That's important: the *sheer joy* of making cinema really comes across in his movies.29 The pleasure shines through, like the elation that Hayao Miyazaki's characters experience when they fly for the first time. You really can tell when a filmmaker is having a great time making their film: you can see it in *Citizen Kane*, in *Close Encounters of the Third Kind*, in *Crouching Tiger. Hidden Dragon*, in *An American In Paris*, in *Once Upon a Time In China*. You can see the filmmakers letting their imaginations unfurl, and that helps to inspire the rest of the creative team to do better work.

Animation is a long, hard slog – very labour intensive, with projects like feature films typically taking three or four years to complete. It takes a particular kind of individual, then, to maintain a high level of enthusiasm and interest. Stanley Kubrick spoke of keeping hold of his initial inspiration for making a movie all the way through the long process of development, pre-production, shooting, post-production and distribution. You have to hang on to whatever it was that really excited you about doing the project in the first place.

There comes a moment during a movie's production when logic has to fly out of the window, and you have to rely on your subconscious. You have to become desperate, Hayao Miyazaki said, you have to think it's not going to work, that you can't solve the problems. At that point of desperation and hardship, the subconscious mind helps out and 'lo and behold an answer comes' (SP, 429-430).

Once a production starts up, it takes on a life of its own, Hayao Miyazaki explained, and his job was to find the way that the movie wants to work, to find the direction it wants to take. As Miyazaki put it – and this also happened with *Spirited Away*:

---
29 Hayao Miyazaki had to feel excited about his work in animation: 'I never want to lose the excitement I experience when I'm working' (SP, 386). Boredom is to be avoided: 'If you watch something for three minutes, you feel like you know everything about it, even what went on backstage, and then you don't feel like watching the rest' (SP, 55).

> The film tries to become a film. The filmmaker just becomes a slave to the film. The relationship is not one of me creating the film, but rather of the film forcing me to create it. (SP, 430)

Although you might have to draw explosions as an animator, Hayao Miyazaki said, the most important thing was to be interested in people, 'in how they live, and in how they interact with things' (SP, 125). Animators aren't just actors, Miyazaki also stated (in 1988), they have to know how to analyze, fuse and put into sequence movements 'involving gravity and momentum, elasticity, perspective, timing, and the fundamental properties of fluids' (SP, 74).

It's no good relying on technique, Hayao Miyazaki said, because it wouldn't help to say something if you don't really have anything to say. Rather, 'technique is something people develop in order to express something' (SP, 145).

Hayao Miyazaki encourages his animators to look, look, look – at the real world, and at real people. Toshio Suzuki has spoken of Miyazaki's incredible facility for observation and recording the real world. To the point where a scene that Miyazaki witnessed years before might crop up in a movie.

> To observe and imitate is most important. He reads books, observes, etc. He often says "Don't rush for a drawing reference book – it should be inside your head".

So Hayao Miyazaki, and the key people in his creative teams – Isao Takahata, Toshio Suzuki, Yoshifumi Kondo, Michiyo Yasuda – are going to be tough, hardworking and determined individuals. Just to complete an animated feature film is achievement enough, but to make pictures that are so exquisite and visionary, is truly mind-boggling.

In 1987, Hayao Miyazaki described the typical animator as young, good-natured, and poor. They made less than 100,000 Yen a month (= $1000). They were paid 400 Yen ($4) a page for theatrical movies and 150 Yen ($1.50) a page for TV animation. Miyazaki reckoned there were about 2,500 animators in Japan (SP, 135). His first wages in animation was 19,000 Yen a month in 1963, Miyazaki said, when he started at Toei Animation.

In all of his lectures and writings, Hayao Miyazaki emphasized the sheer struggle of producing animation.[30] It is an industry for workaholics, to the point where Miyazaki stated: 'without workaholics, Japan's animation could never be sustained' (SP, 187). It is hard work all the way,[31] and there is no way of creating it without months of labour:

> once we start production, it's at full throttle. The schedule is always tight. I urge the staff to take no breaks, to draw, to run, while whipping myself along as well.

Miyazaki remarked in 1987 (SP, 138). It means checking all of the frames and key animation, if possible (SP, 183). 'Works of art are created by those who are prepared to go to the limit,' asserted Miyazaki (1991).

And for Hayao Miyazaki, pursuing animation means pursuing perfection – or something as good as one can produce. 'One has to pursue it until one is satisfied' (SP, 204). When he made *Heidi, Girl of the Alps,* Miyazaki said: 'we worked at a ferocious pace. Due to lack of sleep and fatigue, we were under such stress that we didn't even catch colds' (SP, 137). And sometimes he slept on the floor in the studio: this was more common in Japanese animation in those days than one would think: it wasn't unknown for animators to stay at work all day, and sleep there too, getting up to carry on. I would imagine that today the intensive, workaholic nature of animation is still prevalent, despite unions, labour laws and all the rest.

---

[30] It's worth getting the DVD release of *Spirited Away* because it has the Nippon television special about the making of the movie, and you get some idea of the sheer slog of working in animation.
[31] For Hayao Miyazaki, work is all about passion and effort (SP, 385).

Animated films cannot be made as easily as live-action films [Hayao Miyazaki explained]. I can't be like John Ford, who made more than 100 films, sometimes without even participating in editing his own work. Imagine me directing at this studio for two or three hours, then moving on to another studio to direct a scene like 'there, now the pig gets on the tank,' and then moving on to draw *Nausicaä* – that's just not possible. I don't do things that way, and I don't want to. Animation just doesn't work that way by nature, and if we think it can work that way then we are finished.

THE PROCESS.

In the Japanese animation industry, the script comes first. Storyboards and image boards are drawn when the script is completed (but sometimes before then). The storyboards are called *e-conte* (a combination of *ei*, picture, and continuity). Hayao Miyazaki likes to draw the storyboards himself.

Once the film is complete in terms of storyboards, plus indications of dialogue and sound effects, it goes to the key animators: they put the movie together in terms of the key animation (the animation at the beginning and the end of an action). In-between work means animating the movements between the key frames which the key animators have drawn, using time sheets. At the same time, the drawings are cleaned up.

Once the drawings have been completed, they are transferred to cels (celluloid), and inked and painted. Finally, they are photographed (a whole complex process in itself). Photographic and special effects may be added at this stage. As expected, Hayao Miyazaki likes to check every stage in the process.[32]

It has been a regular occurrence for Hayao Miyazaki to be storyboarding a movie while it's in production, as well as producing image-boards. That's not too much of a problem in

---

[32] However, animation doesn't always use 24 frames per second, called 'ones': it often goes to 'twos' (12 frames a second) or 'threes' (8 frames per second). Even Miyazaki's latest movies use those frame rates.

live-action, when storyboards are often cast aside anyway when the filmmakers and actors reach the set and rehearse and work out new ways of shooting a scene. In animation, it's much more problematic, because it affects the whole process. On *Laputa: Castle In the Sky,* for example, Miyazaki recalled that he was working on the storyboards throughout production:

> My daily schedule went like this: I got up in the morning, I drew storyboards, I returned to the office. At the office, I touched-up my staff's material. At night, I went home and did some more storyboards. After that, I slept. In Japan, I'm afraid the only one who makes animation this way is me, since no one else could take it. (1987a)

Hayao Miyazaki doesn't need a script, Isao Takahata explained, and he doesn't even bother to complete the storyboards before launching into production (2009, 458). All he needs is a clear idea of his characters[33] and the imagined world he's building. As overseen by Miyazaki, Takahata said that the production 'starts to take on the elements of an endlessly improvised performance'. And he liked to work on every process in a production at the same time, instead of waiting for one part to be complete.[34] It was as if Miyazaki 'were trying to turn the creative process into an erotic adventure', Takahata said (2009, 458).

One of the chief reasons for Hayao Miyazaki concentrating much more on the storyboards or continuity sketches for his own movies, rather than on producing a script, or even writing out the original story, was time: *Laputa: Castle In the Sky* required 650 sketches, *Kiki's Delivery Service* 550 and *Whisper of the Heart* 450 (SP, 103). With all that work to do,

---
[33] Because he works with his characters for such a long time during production, Isao Takahata remarked, Miyazaki has to identify with them emotionally (2009, 456).
[34] There is no set way of making a movie, Hayao Miyazaki asserted: it didn't have to develop from ideas to script to image boards to storyboards to animation. All of those events could be taking place at the same time, or in a different order (SP, 58).

there just wasn't time to write the screenplay.35

And Hayao Miyazaki said he couldn't work that way anyway: 'I've tried writing the story out many times before, but even if I think a story works great in text, when we render it in continuity sketches it's usually unusable' (SP, 103).

It is standard procedure in Japanese animation to record the voice tracks after the animation has been completed (rather as European movies dub on the voices later, as was Federico Fellini's habit). It's the other way around in the Western animation tradition, with animators using pre-recorded voice tracks for part of their inspiration (it is common for animators to employ video recordings of the actors performing the script, and also to draw on the actor in other work).

Toshio Suzuki described the casting process for voices in Hayao Miyazaki's movies:

> Miyazaki does not watch TV or films, so he doesn't know many actors. When we have meetings with the casting director, Miyazaki's suggestions for actors are usually dead! Especially for older characters like Old-Sophie [in *Howl's Moving Castle*]. So I usually come up with a list. We all listen to the tapes together, and Miyazaki makes the final decision. They are not always professional voice-actors.36

Hayao Miyazaki dislikes the Western practice, developed famously at the Walt Disney Company, of using live-action photography as a reference or a starting-point for animation. Miyazaki hates the technique. It doesn't work, Miyazaki reckoned, and pointed to the overly expressive and unnatural movements of Disney characters such as Cinderella and Snow White, who look like they're acting in a ballet. It was no good using a young American woman as a model in pursuing realism; even more of the symbolism of the fairy tales was

---

35 As Ingmar Bergman noted: 'I write scripts to serve as skeletons awaiting the flesh and sinew of images' (*The New York Times,* January 22, 1978).
36 Miyazaki has said that he does know of some of the actors that Suzuki has suggested, and he does watch TV and movies.

lost (SP, 75).

And animation and visual effects in the West is still locked into the notion of using live-action reference material: films like *Avatar* and *The Lord of the Rings* have used motion capture technology to drive the animation of their characters (and crowed about it in the publicity).

In Japan, Hayao Miyazaki preferred his animators not to become slaves to live-action photography: if they do, 'their enjoyment of their work plummets by half' (SP, 75).

MIYAZAKI'S MOVIES AND JAPAN

The films of Hayao Miyazaki and Studio Ghibli are truly a phenomenon in Japan. Every time a movie by Hayao Miyazaki is released in theatres, everyone in Japan goes to see it. Or that's what it feels like: in short, every Miyazaki movie since *Porco Rosso* has been the top film that year: *Princess Mononoke*, *Spirited Away*, *Howl's Moving Castle*, and *Ponyo On the Cliff By the Sea*. And not just the top grossing movie, but the picture that beats all the other movies by a huge proportion. For example, in 2004, the year when big American movies *Harry Potter and the Prisoner of Azkaban*, *The Lord of the Rings: The Return of the King* and *Spider-man 2* were released in Japan, *Howl's Moving Castle* was the top film by a long way (in 2003, the biggest movie worldwide was *The Lord of the Rings*, and in 2004 it was *Harry Potter 3*).

From *Princess Mononoke* onwards, Hayao Miyazaki's movies have had very wide releases in Japan: 348 screens for *Princess Mononoke*, 336 screens for *Spirited Away*, and 450 screens for *Howl's Moving Castle* (compare that with the 3,000 or more screens for releases in the U.S.A.). *Princess Mononoke* was the most financially successful Japanese film up to that point, in Japan itself, and including all releases, not just animation. Only *The Passion of the Christ* was more successful than *Spirited Away* as a foreign language movie worldwide (and *The Passion of the Christ* is a true oddity, being an American religious movie filmed in dead languages – Latin and Aramaic).

Hayao Miyazaki has said that he is most concerned with how his movies are received in Japan: Japan is the primary market for Miyazaki's pictures (culturally as well as financially). 'I'm only worried about how my film would be viewed in Japan. Frankly, I don't worry too much about how it plays elsewhere,' Miyazaki told CNN in 1999.[37]

Hayao Miyazaki was not an English speaker,[38] and relied on other people to translate and dub his movies. His chief concern was with the Japanese audience: he hoped that the translations and dubs of his pictures would be accurate. That was the main thing – to stay true to the movie as it was intended to be seen. That most especially applied to the dictum: *no cuts*.

Hayao Miyazaki didn't want to make movies for fans who only wanted one sort of movie. It was no good for film producers to categorize fans, Miyazaki remarked in 1989, and only make films for that kind of person.

Hayao Miyazaki warned against viewers watching his movies over and over. It was no good getting obsessed with a film, Miyazaki insisted: to a friend who said his child had watched *Princess Mononoke* over 50 times, Miyazaki sent him a letter:

> saying he was making a terrible mistake. Once a year, maybe once a lifetime, is really how often you should see any of my films.... Owning a little puppy will teach you a lot more about life than watching *Totoro* 100 times.[39]

The sentiment recalls British actor Alec Guinness, who

---
[37] CNN, *Today*, Oct 3, 1997.
[38] According to Lonely Planet's *Japan* guidebook, few Japanese can speak English as well as most Europeans, or Hong Kong Chinese, or Singaporeans, or Indians (C. Rowthorn, 2007, 50).
[39] Quoted in S. Fritz, 1999.

was hounded by obsessive *Star Wars* fans. Guinness recounted meeting a boy in San Francisco who said he had seen *Star Wars* over 100 times. When Guinness asked the boy to promise never to see *Star Wars* again, he burst into tears. His mother, indignant, barked 'what a dreadful thing to say to a child!'. Guinness commented: 'I just hope the lad, now in his thirties, is not living in a fantasy world of second-hand, childish banalities'.[40]

In his writings collected in *Starting Point*, Hayao Miyazaki repeatedly complains about the current state of animation, in movies and on TV. But he doesn't have rose-tinted glasses on: animated shows weren't better in the 'old days', either: it was just that there were far fewer of them, so each one stood out more.

As well as the sorry state of current animation, Hayao Miyazaki also thinks there is *too much* animation around today, and too many channels on TV, too much of everything. So it was impossible to judge if anything was any good anymore, because viewers were inundated with it. And it also meant that animators were more over-worked than ever before, having to satisfy television's insatiable demand for more material.

In 2005, there were 430 *animé* production studios in Japan, and most of them were in Tokyo. (And that's one of the reasons why so many *animé* shows are set in Tokyo, including some of Hayao Miyazaki's films). The *animé* market was worth about ¥20 billion ($200m) in 2004.

The typical 30 minute *animé* TV show cost 10 million Yen. (There are about 100 Yen to the US dollar, so 10 million Yen is about $100,000). Thus, Hayao Miyazaki's movies are very high budget movies, in Japanese *animé* terms, not only compared to TV shows, but also compared with animated feature films: the budget of *Spirited Away* was in the region of ¥1.9-2.5 billion, or $19-25 million US dollars. So Miyazaki's

---
[40] A. Guinness, *A Positively Final Appearance*, Penguin, London, 1998

pictures are some of the most expensive in Japanese animation history, and in Japanese film history.[41]

But $19m or $25m is still a lot cheaper than the American equivalent (and $1 million for *Nausicaä of the Valley of the Wind* in 1984 is a bargain): the animated Disney and Pixar movies of recent times have included the following budgets: *Tarzan* $115m (or $142m or $150m, depending on sources); *Treasure Planet* $140m; *Ratatouille* $150m; and *Home On the Range* $110m.

These figures aren't really helpful, because movie budgets are notoriously difficult to check accurately: no one wants to admit how much money something *really* cost, or *exactly* how much they're earning (and Hollywood studios routinely exaggerate figures like budgets and grosses). But you know if the budgets are one hundred million dollars or more, then *somebody somewhere* is making a lot of money. As William Goldman, noted, there's a lot of money to be had in simply *making* a film, regardless of whether it's released or seen or not. And some people make a living out of producing movies, including existing on development deals and other deals, and many of those films aren't shot, and some that *are* filmed aren't released.

It's hard to believe that movies like *Home On the Range* or *Tarzan* from the Mouse House could have cost over $110 million or $115 million, but there are all sorts of economic factors to consider. The piece-work labour of Japanese *animé* is going to be cheaper than hiring staff on a permanent basis that occurs more in American animation.[42] Living costs, unions and working conditions in Japan and America are further factors. The much longer production schedules of American animated movies must contribute to the higher costs too: Hayao Miyazaki and his teams delivered *Nausicaä of*

---

[41] The only reason that theatrical movies are often better than TV animation was budget, Hayao Miyazaki asserted (SP, 55), but it didn't matter to him whether he made TV movies or theatrical movies.

[42] Miyazaki often complained about the piecework system of producing animation in Japan, which turned out work like an assembly line, instead of the handcrafted and personal, artistic approach that Miyazaki favoured.

the Valley of the Wind and Laputa: Castle In the Sky in less than a year, while Disney and Pixar movies can take 3 or more years. However, the large crews of hundreds of workers aren't hired for all of those years, but it's safe to say that the production teams in American (and Western) feature animation are larger than those in the Japanese animation industry, and that they are hired for longer periods. All of which drives costs up (at the same time, Western animation companies farm out work to outfits in countries such as Korea, Thailand and India, just as the Japanese animation industry does).

There are a number of reasons why Hayao Miyazaki can command such high budgets for his movies: one is the simple fact that, from his first film *The Castle of Cagliostro* onwards, his movies have made money. And the later ones, such as *Porco Rosso* or *Princess Mononoke*, have been hugely successful. Miyazaki has had the top grossing movie in Japan a number of times: *Porco Rosso*, *Princess Mononoke*, *Spirited Away*, and *Howl's Moving Castle*. That means his films can attract a lot of investment. Other reasons would include prestige: Miyazaki's movies are very high quality pictures, works of art in themselves, so that glory is reflected back on the investors (as in 'look at us, we put money into *Spirited Away*').

I would imagine that hiring Hayao Miyazaki to make a film is also a bargain: you are going to get a workaholic and perfectionist who will do all he can to make his movie the best it can possibly be. Miyazaki isn't the kind of film director to shuffle on set late, mumble a couple of words, then retire to his trailer to loaf about for the rest of the day. As a producer himself, Miyazaki is going to stay with the movie until it's completed.

※

Like the films of Yasujiro Ozu or Kenji Mizoguchi or Akira Kurosawa, the films of Hayao Miyazaki are very *Japanese* –

they are set in Japan, draw on Japanese history and culture,[43] and are about Japanese subjects (even when they're set in or about Europe).[44] But they are also – like the movies of Yasujiro Ozu, Kenji Mizoguchi and Akira Kurosawa – films which can and do travel around the world.

Most films don't. Most movies don't get released or shown outside their country of origin. Hayao Miyazaki's movies are both very Japanese and very international. Only a few filmmakers achieve that kind of flexibility.

Hayao Miyazaki is sometimes dubbed 'the Japanese Disney'; Helen McCarthy makes another suggestion, more in tune with Miyazaki's hands-on artistry: 'the Kurosawa of Japanese animation' (2002, 10). Kurosawa is of course the giant of Japanese cinema: there is a marvellous series of interviews between Miyazaki and Kurosawa, which are highly recommended. (*My Neighbor Totoro* was one of Kurosawa's 100 favourite films; he loved the Cat-bus; Kurosawa said he wept watching *Kiki's Delivery Service;* and he also said that Miyazaki's movies were more important than his own).

Other notable filmmakers in Japanese cinema, apart from the *sensei*[45] himself (Akira Kurosawa) include: Yasujiro Ozu, Kenji Mizoguchi, and Ichikawa Kon, and Japanese New Wave directors, such as Nagisa Oshima, Hiroshi Teshigahara, Masashiro Shinoda, Takeshi Kitano and Yoshishige Yoshida.

Among the classic films of Japanese cinema are: *Tokyo Story, The Flavour of Green Tea Over Rice, The Life of Oharu, Ohayu, Sansho Dayu, Kwaidan, Early Summer, Woman of the Dunes, Ugetsu Monogatari,* and *Ai No Corrida* (*In the Realm of the Senses*). And of course, *anything* by Akira Kurosawa (even

---

43 Miyazaki drew on Japanese history, ancient Japanese court tales, sci-fi, fairy tales, and mythology.

44 Although Hayao Miyazaki's cinema employs a huge input from European culture, history and landscapes, his films are always Japanese. Even the ones set in European places, like *Porco Rosso* or *Kiki's Delivery Service*, are very, very Japanese.

45 Miyazaki doesn't like the word *sensei*, and persuades people not to use it. He has said: 'I am an animator. I feel like I'm the manager of an animation cinema factory. I am not an executive. I'm rather like a foreman, like the boss of a team of craftsmen. That is the spirit of how I work.'

one of Kurosawa's minor films is finer than many filmmakers' best efforts).

Hayao Miyazaki ranks up there with the great Japanese filmmakers, I would say. Only a few filmmakers reach those heights, but Miyazaki can rightly be placed alongside Kenji Mizoguchi, Yasujiro Ozu and Akira Kurosawa. Miyazaki does everything that a great filmmaker can do or should do – and then he does something extra, that magical or special element that raises very good art to the status of great art.

That extra or magical or mysterious or added ingredient is a combination of (1) compassion and humanity, (2) a world vision which includes *everything*, *every* aspect of life, and (3) an ability to embrace and celebrate all forms of life (in Miyazaki's case, the natural world as well as the human realm).

Or, to put it another way: the films of Hayao Miyazaki are far, far above your regular, average movie. They are special, highly individual, very unusual, and deeply moving. To achieve that in any medium is *very* difficult. To do it with painted pieces of plastic seems particularly amazing. Once again, let's not forget that Miyazaki is not working alone, but has a huge team of collaborators, some young and new to the business, and some who have worked with him for decades.

CELS VERSUS COMPUTERS

The films of Hayao Miyazaki are traditional cel animation, but computers and computer-generated effects and devices are employed from time to time. In *Princess Mononoke*, Studio Ghibli began to use computers, but only in small amounts. For instance, computers were used for the time-consuming process of ink and paint for about 10,000 cels (the intention was to use the computer for around 5,000 cels, but with deadlines approaching, the production resorted to more computer work). However, there were some 140,000 cels used in *Princess Mononoke*, so the computer was used to ink and paint less than 10% of the cels. *Princess Mononoke* has around 1600 shots or scenes (in Japanese animation, shots are also called cuts or scenes).

Studio Ghibli's movies, though, never look computerized or digital, because by the far the bulk is conventional (hand-drawn) cel animation. However, cel animation in movies is as supremely *technological* and *industrial* as computers or digital technology. *Everything* in movies is *technological*, everything is fake, everything is a highly sophisticated cultural form created by humans for mass entertainment. So whether it's done with machines like cameras or pencils or paintbrushes or computers isn't really the point.

It *is* important, though, I think, that Hayao Miyazaki's films don't have the plasticky look of computer-generated imagery, or the 3-D look of computer animation, or the floaty appearance of computerized additions to scenes. For instance, since the mid-1990s and the success of *Toy Story*, animated movies have shifted towards what's termed 3-D (a misleading term, as all of animation is always two dimensional, when it's projected on a screen. It's more a technical term, referring to the use of 3-D models and devices inside computer programmes, and the simulation of 3-D with the use of 3-D goggles for viewing movies). But Miyazaki's works are refreshingly *not* like the 3-D animation that's seen in many animated movies from *Toy Story* onwards: all of Pixar's output, plus *Ice Age, Robots, Shrek, Chicken Little*, etc.[46]

It's significant, too, that Hayao Miyazaki's pictures don't employ digital additions to scenes which don't really mesh with traditional 2-D animation. For instance, Disney's *Treasure Planet, Atlantis, The Rescuers Down Under* and Warner Bros' *The Iron Man* have used computer-generated (3-D)

---

[46] Miyazaki remarked in 2005: 'I think 2-D animation disappeared from Disney because they made so many uninteresting films. They became very conservative in the way they created them. It's too bad. I thought 2-D and 3-D could coexist happily.'

elements placed into hand-drawn (but probably computer-inked) 2-D animation. The digital elements often look floaty and disconnected to the rest of the scenes.

However, using computers is just another tool out of many that animation employs: a common view, still being voiced by critics who should know better, is that:

cel animation = good, computer animation = bad.

Rubbish – *all* animation is *already* highly technological. Film critics really should visit film studios from time to time, to dispel the falsehoods that they perpetuate. For instance, that some movie sets look made out of cardboard: actually, *all* movie sets are constructed from bits of wood or foam or cardboard and painted, then they're torn down as soon as shooting stops on them.

If you visited an animation house in Tokyo, London, or Hollywood (or the many out-sourced centres in, say, India or Korea), you'd find tons of technology and machines, with computers being just one among multitudes. For instance, the cameras employed to photograph the cels are very sophisticated. And they always have been: have a look at the famous multiplane camera designed by William Garity at the Walt Disney Company in Burbank in the 1930s, which required a group of technicians to operate it.

The cel vs. CGI argument merely trots out the ancient oppositions between old and new, or tradition and modernism.

Hayao Miyazaki thought it was too late for him to convert to CGI and computers; he thought that hand-drawn animation would never die out: there would always be someone producing it in a garage somewhere.

MIYAZAKI AND DISNEY

As inventive, imaginative cinema, Hayao Miyazaki's films are second to none: *Laputa: Castle In the Sky*, *Kiki's Delivery Service*, *Porco Rosso*, *Spirited Away*, *Princess Mononoke* and *Howl's Moving Castle*. Miyazaki's cinema is marked by incredible fantasy worlds, which always remained grounded in recognizable realities; magical beings; action-packed adventures; the most astonishing portrayals of flight and flying machines in cinema; secret worlds and hidden dimensions; a passionate evocation of the wonders of the natural world, with a mystical reverence for elemental forces (embodied in animal spirits, or trees, or water, or clouds, or dragons); eccentric minor characters (with powerful, crazy old women and crusty old men a speciality); and young people (often girls) as the central characters. Miyazaki's films are very optimistic and life-affirming,[47] and celebrate the joy of being alive.

And, not least, Hayao Miyazaki's films are among the most technically breathtaking animated movies ever made. They are instantly recognizable as a Miyazaki or Studio Ghibli product – no one else makes movies like this. So many of these qualities would endear themselves to the makers of Disney films.

Walt Disney Company's *Atlantis* (2001) seemed to be very obviously influenced by Hayao Miyazaki (sometimes dubbed 'the Japanese Disney'), and Studio Ghibli. As well as *Atlantis*, other movies in the late Victorian steam-punk style would include *The League of Extraordinary Gentlemen* (2003), *Hell-Boy* (2004), *The Golden Compass* (2007),[48] and *Steamboy* (2004), Katsuhiro Otomo's long-delayed but disappointing follow-up to his stupendous *Akira*. Pixar/ Disney's computer animated movie *Up* (Pete Docter and Bob Peterson, 2008) is

---
47 Isao Takahata described Miyazaki as someone 'who never runs from or slacks off at work, who hates defeatism and who is always optimistic' (2009, 455).
48 The fiction of Philip Pullman, including his most famous work, the *His Dark Materials* trilogy, is set in a fantasy of late Victorian Britain to early 20th century.

among the most Miyazakian of recent Disney works.

However, Hayao Miyazaki has also critiqued the pandering of Disney's movies to the lowest common denominator: there must be some kind of purity of feeling in a movie, even the popular and mainstream ones. They might invite anyone in, 'but the barriers to exit must be high and purifying' (SP, 72). For Miyazaki:

> Films must also not be produced out of idle nervousness or boredom, or be used to recognize, emphasize, or amplify true vulgarity. And in that context, I must say that I hate Disney's works. The barrier to both the entry and exit of Disney films is too low and too wide. To me, they show nothing but contempt for the audience. (SP, 72)

The Walt Disney corporation itself has been involved in many of Hayao Miyazaki's films – producing the English language versions, including *Spirited Away*, as well as distributing them in Western territories via its Buena Vista distribution arm[49] (the deal was made in 1996 between Disney and Tokuma, the publishing company that owned Studio Ghibli). However, the Disney corporation does not handle Ghibli's merchandising, which would seem a perfect fit at first. But Ghibli and Tokuma have held onto merchandizing rights.[50] And they haven't allowed computer games to be produced from Ghibli movies.

---

[49] Prior to the deal with Disney, Studio Ghibli had been approached by Fox and Warners. The chief reason that Disney was selected as an overseas distribution partner for Ghibli was that it agreed to the stipulation that nothing would be cut from Ghibli's movies. Fox and Warners hadn't agreed to that, according to Toshio Suzuki.

[50] According to Helen McCarthy, Hayao Miyazaki is not much interested in merchandizing or having his movies distributed outside of Japan. Those issues are 'completely unimportant. To him, the movies themselves, seen full-size in the cinema, are the only things that count' (M, 211).

JAPANESE AND ENGLISH

Another striking aspect of Hayao Miyazaki's films is the success of the English language versions. As anyone who's watched a few non-English movies will know, some dubbing can be terrible, produced with barely any care at all. The first time audiences in the West will have seen a Miyazaki movie, including *Spirited Away*, will probably be in a dubbed version (they are favoured by TV broadcasters, for instance: if there's a choice, a broadcaster will always go with a dubbed version). The first movie by Miyazaki I saw was *Laputa: Castle In the Sky* in the Walt Disney dubbed version; my son Jake and I watched the movie and were amazed by it.

A number of companies (such as New World Pictures, Streamline Pictures, and Manga Video) have dubbed Hayao Miyazaki's and Studio Ghibli's movies, but it is definitely the Walt Disney Company which has made the English dubbing their own. And Disney have done it so well (many of their versions are overseen by veteran Jack Fletcher).[51] Miyazaki's films have been given the high-class treatment, with big name actors voicing the characters: Michael Keaton, Claire Danes, Jean Simmons, Christian Bale, Lauren Bacall, Jade Pinkett Smith, etc. (The principles of casting voices for animation are different from live-action, of course, but look at those names – they are still well-known actors, and also primarily American).

This also happened with *Spirited Away*, which included Daveigh Chase, Suzanne Pleshette, Jason Marsden, Susan Egan, Lauren Holly, Michael Chiklis, and character actors like David Ogden Stiers, John Ratzenberger and Jack Angel.[52] For

---

[51] As well as John Lasseter, Rick Dempsey has been involved with many of the Disney versions of Hayao Miyazaki's movies, as producer and dialogue director, and also David Candiff as production manager, with casting by Ned Lott and voice direction by Jack Fletcher.

[52] You might recognize some of the voice cast used among the secondary characters in the Walt Disney versions of Hayao Miyazaki's movies, as they appear in many animations, from Disney, Pixar and other studios: David Ogden Stiers, John Ratzenberger, Jack Angel, John Hostetter, Tress MacNeille, Sherry Lynn, Phil Hartman, Tony Jay, and Cloris Leachman.

the Walt Disney Company, Hayao Miyazaki's movies are prestige projects – but they also sell well (though not nearly as well as in Japan, where they are the equivalent of a *Titanic* or an *Avatar* in terms of box office).

The English language versions have altered Hayao Miyazaki's films, however, by changing some of the lines of dialogue, or adding lines (not to mention the vocal performance itself). Most Western, English-speaking audiences probably prefer the English dubbed versions (though I prefer the Japanese versions in all cases).

For instance, there are many differences between the English subtitles – which presumably translate the Japanese dialogue (though not all of it) – and the English dubbed versions. There are lines in the English subtitles which don't appear in the English dubbed version – and vice versa. Background sounds and additional lines of dialogue are also added; thus they are *not* the original sound mixes – and the sound, as many filmmakers have noted, can be 90% of what's going on in a movie. This means that Studio Ghibli's films have a slightly different impact in their Japanese subtitled and English dubbed versions (regardless of where they are screened).[53]

---

[53] Also, some companies have re-edited movies such as *The Castle of Cagliostro* to get rid of Japanese words and credits.

#3

ASPECTS OF HAYAO MIYAZAKI'S CINEMA

MOVIES FOR EVERYONE

A significant element in Hayao Miyazaki's cinema is that it doesn't talk down to its audience. It takes its fantastical scenarios seriously – but also allows for humour and silliness. His films are not patronizing, but also not lecturing or hectoring. Pedagogical, yes, but not over-zealous, or hitting the audience over the head with moralizing.

Hayao Miyazaki's movies, like all great fantasy movies, are not (just) for children, but for people of all ages. In fact, like fairy tales, their primary audience is not children at all, but adults. Children don't write fairy tales, don't publish books, and don't make fantasy films. Adults do. And fairy tales always were for adults, until the 19th century, when they became part of the commodification of childhood.[54]

But originally, and for always, fairy tales have been written *by adults, for adults*. Similarly with fantasy movies. That's not to say that the films of Hayao Miyazaki and his teams are not enjoyed by children, and do not contain elements that address children directly. And of course Miyazaki's films often feature children or young people as their heroes.

Working for children meant *beginnings*: for children,

---

[54] See any of the excellent books by Jack Zipes in the bibliography on this topic.

something is new for the first time: the first time you took a train journey by yourself (like Chihiro in *Spirited Away*). Miyazaki explained:

> The single difference between films for children and films for adults is that in films for children, there is always the option to start again, to create a new beginning. In films for adults, there are no ways to change things. What happened, happened.

Hayao Miyazaki did not make movies wholly for children, but his desire to entertain children was certainly vital: 'I try to create what I wanted to see when I was a child, or what I believe my own children want to see' (SP, 50). However, he also acknowledged that producing movies for children can be even more challenging than producing movies for adults, because 'they deal with origins and fundamentals' (SP, 91).

> When I hear talk of children's futures, I just get upset, because the future of a child is to become a boring adult. Children have only the moment. In that moment, an individual child is gradually passing through the state of childhood... but there are children in existence all the time. 55

Being a parent was certainly a spur to Hayao Miyazaki wanting to make pictures for children. Why? Because, he said in a 1995 interview, when you have a child of three, you want to show it something good. And when you see there is nothing good enough out there, you have to make a movie yourself (SP, 432).

Detractors would probably trot out the same criticisms of

---

55 Quoted in A. Osmond, 2008, 20.

Hayao Miyazaki's cinema as they do of Walt Disney's films,[56] or children's book authors: they would see only that Miyazaki's movies are very colourful and stylized and so can't be 'serious' or 'important'. They would say that Miyazaki's films are intended for children, and so can't be as serious or as valuable as films by, say, Ingmar Bergman or Wong Kar-wai. They would say that Miyazaki's pictures are 'lightweight' or light-hearted, as if the only kind of serious movies have to be heavily melancholy or dramatic or tragic. And finally they would complain that Miyazaki's pictures are fantasies, and fantasy doesn't have the cultural kudos of Shakespearean or Sophoclean tragedy.

All junk, of course.

A recurring theme in Hayao Miyazaki's writings is the ambition to make something for children that's meaningful and special, that has more value than the run-of-the-mill animation on television (SP, 187). 'I want to create works that children can enjoy, or that they can spend some quality time with', Miyazaki asserted (SP, 55).

All adults were children once, and that is partly what Hayao Miyazaki's movies trade on: not childishness so much as a return to a child-like view of the world – which includes wonder and awe as well as fear and anxiety. In this respect, Miyazaki's cinema shares much with Disney's cinema, or many of the great filmmakers who have taken children or young people as their protagonists.

Most of the Walt Disney Studios' films since the revival of the Disney Studios in 1984 by Michael Eisner, Frank Wells and Jeffrey Katzenberg have been what I call 'dual track' or multi-layered movies. That is, pictures which simultaneously target different segments of the audience: action and knockabout

---

[56] Miyazaki, like many filmmakers, takes a dim view of critics and reviews, but values audiences: 'I never read reviews. I'm not interested. But I value a lot the reactions of the spectators'. However, a filmmaker can't just do *anything* he likes. 'I think it's impossible to do everything you want', Miyazaki claimed. 'You have to make such a movie in a different place from a movie which one or two million people pay to see and get satisfied. When I watch a movie such as Tarkovsky's *Stalker*, I feel 'this SOB is doing as he pleases!' I think he is such a talented guy.'

comedy for the kids, and knowing, self-conscious quips and in-jokes for the adults. Actually, Uncle Walt knew all about that, about how to talk to parents and their offspring at the same time.

But the films of Hayao Miyazaki and his teams are not like that. They don't split up the audience, and they don't wink at the audience (or at the adult members of the audience). Miyazaki's movies are not self-conscious or 'postmodern' or cleverly allusive of other movies. Oh, they draw on other films often, but they don't do superficial *hommages* or spoofs of other movies. They don't deliver those in-jokes and clever satires of other films, which are so much a part of the Hollywood family movie.

Contemporary animated films are stuffed with those allusions and pop culture references: *Finding Nemo, Chicken Little, Cars, Ice Age,* and, most notoriously, the *Shrek* series.[57] But *Laputa: Castle In the Sky, Porco Rosso* and *Spirited Away* don't contain those silly references to the rolling boulder in *Raiders of the Lost Art,* or Norman Bates in *Psycho,* or the shark in *Jaws,* or numerous quotations from pop music. Hayao Miyazaki and his teams are too busy telling the story in their films to stop for jokes about *E.T.* or martial arts movies. They don't want to take you out of the story with bitter snipes at Disney or DreamWorks or Fox or Warners, or turning the film halfway through into a dumb TV game show. They are not, in short, theme park movies, consumer movies, commodified movies, or pop culture movies.

While contemporary Hollywood cinema endlessly cannibalizes itself (remakes on top of sequels on top of remakes – when was the last time you saw an American movie based on an *original idea* released in a theatre, not on DVD or TV?),

---

[57] DreamWorks' *Shrek* (2001) replayed fairy tale clichés in a knowing, ironic, postmodern and comic fashion. There were many digs at Disney films and the Disney corporation in *Shrek.* It seemed a bit odd, even obsessive, that Jeffrey Katzenberg (via DreamWorks SKG) should still be attacking Disney, his former employers. By the time *Shrek* came out, it was seven years since Katzenberg had departed the Mouse House. Some critics exalt the *Shrek* movies, but you can't even place them beside the films of Hayao Miyazaki.

Hayao Miyazaki's cinema just gets on with making the films and telling a cracking tale. Miyazaki's pictures are boundless when it comes to ideas and inventions.

But the movies of Hayao Miyazaki and his teams are also not deadly serious – they are not po-faced and do not take themselves too seriously, like the films of Andrei Tarkovsky or Carl-Theodor Dreyer. There's just too much warmth and tenderness and *life* in a Miyazaki movie for it to be solemn for too long.

FLIGHT

Flight — the sky — transcendence.

Few filmmakers have been so preoccupied with flying as Hayao Miyazaki (Steven Spielberg is definitely one).[58] One wonders if Miyazaki would really liked to have been a pilot – in World War One, and into the 1920s (just like Porco Rosso). Spielberg remarked:

> I am absolutely fascinated and terrified by flying. It is a big deal in my movies. All my movies have airplanes in them. You name the movie – they all fly. To me, flying is synonymous with freedom and unlimited imagination but, interestingly enough, I'm afraid to fly.[59]

One of the reasons that Hayao Miyazaki is able to include so many flying sequences in his movies is surely cost: a flying

---

[58] Moments of flight in Spielberg's work include the helicopters and flying UFOs in *Close Encounters of the Third Kind*; the airship and planes in the *Indiana Jones* series; the sea plane at the start of *Raiders of the Lost Ark* (plus the unusual German plane which kills one of Indy's adversaries); the planes in *1941*; the magical BMX bike flight in *E.T.*; the fairy tale Peter Pan flying in *Hook*; the flights and pilots in *Always*; the futuristic flying vehicles in *A.I.* and *Minority Report*; the airliners at the airport in *The Terminal*; more jets in *Catch Me If You Can*; and the last image of *Jurassic Park* is of flight (a helicopter and pterodactyls flying over the ocean; *The Lost World* also ends on flight, as a pterodactyl lands on a tree). And Spielberg's WW2 film set in China, where the Japanese are the villains, 1987's *Empire of the Sun,* contains many flying scenes.
[59] Interview with A.M. Bahiana, *Cinema Papers*, Mch, 1992

scene can't be much more costly to produce than other action scenes in animation. But if you had to do those scenes in live-action, they would be much more expensive.

'Alles will schweben',[60] said the German poet Rainer Maria Rilke in his *Sonnets of Orpheus*. All things want to fly. The image of flight is the symbol of transcendence, as the *Pancavimca Brahmana* says: 'he who understands has wings'.[61] Mircea Eliade, the historian of religions, wrote:

> we must always take into consideration the primary experience of the sacrality of the sky and of celestial and atmospheric phenomena. This is one of the few experiences that spontaneously reveal transcendence and majesty. In addition, the ecstatic ascents of shamans, the symbolism of flight, the imaginary experience of altitude as a deliverance from weight, contribute to consecrating the celestial space as supremely the source and dwelling place of superhuman beings: gods, spirits, civilizing heroes. (1979, 27)

Mircea Eliade reckoned that the sky was the first symbol of transcendence, and remains the primary emblem of the sacred, of spirituality, flight, ascension and revelation. The sky is heaven, where the gods live.

> I believe, personally, that it is through consideration of the sky's immensity that man is led to a revelation of transcendence, of the sacred.[62]

And it's not only flying in machines and aeroplanes in Hayao Miyazaki's cinema, although there are 100s of those – many characters fly by themselves, whether it's Totoro, Ponyo, Howl, Sheeta and Pazu (using the crystal) in *Laputa: Castle In the Sky*, or Kiki on her broomstick. And in *Spirited Away*, Yubaba as a bird, the River God and Haku as a dragon.

---
[60] *Sonnets to Orpheus*, tr. J.B. Leishman, Hogarth Press, London, 1946, II, 14. 5.
[61] *Pancavimca Brahmana*, in M. Eliade, 1985, 4.
[62] M. Eliade, 1984, 162.

HAYAO MIYAZAKI AND FEMINISM

Not a few commentators have noted that Hayao Miyazaki is a feminist. At Studio Ghibli, Miyazaki has been concerned about the working conditions for women (the jobs in animation production have traditionally been partly arranged along gender lines: at the Disney Studios in the Classical Hollywood era, for instance, all of the key animators were male, while the inking department, which comprises dull, repetitive work, were largely female). (Japan is still a rather patriarchal society: women earn 66% of what men earn (compared to 76% in the U.S.A., and 83% in Britain), and only 9% of seats in the government (in the Diet)).

Certainly a pro-women stance comes out in Hayao Miyazaki's films, including *Spirited Away*, in the roles that he and his writers assign to women (his mother is the source of inspiration for many aspects of his female characters, according to Dan Cavallaro [29]). Second wave feminists and third wave feminists could likely criticize the films of Miyazaki and his teams on numerous counts in their portrayal of women. But it's certainly significant that so many of Miyazaki's protagonists are female. You can search through the work of many of Miyazaki's contemporaries and struggle to find movies with a female lead. But *Nausicaä of the Valley of the Wind*, *My Neighbor Totoro*, *Kiki's Delivery Service*, *Howl's Moving Castle* and of course *Spirited Away* have female characters as the chief protagonist.[63] And it's not only Miyazaki's films, but those of Studio Ghibli: *Whisper of the Heart*, *The Cat Returns* and *Only Yesterday* have women in the main roles, while *Grave of the Fireflies* is about a boy and a girl.

The people who put together Rosso's plane in *Porco Rosso* are all women (a plane factory's traditionally a male preserve, as is the metalworks where the women work in

---

[63] In *Laputa: Castle In the Sky,* both Pazu and Sheeta are the heroes, in *Ponyo On the Cliff By the Sea* it's Ponyo and Sosuke, and in *Princess Mononoke* it's Ashitaka and San.

Irontown in *Princess Mononoke*), and the workers in the bathhouse in *Spirited Away* are women (there are men there too – but they are giant frogs, which's somehow apt).

For instance, only two of Steven Spielberg's pictures have women as the main character: *The Color Purple* and *The Sugarland Express*; none of George Lucas's films; one of Tim Burton's films (*Alice in Wonderland*); and only two of Francis Coppola's movies (*Peggy Sue Got Married* and *The Rain People*, though his entry in *New York Stories* would also count). Some Western filmmakers, of course, have specialized in creating stories with women in the lead: Woody Allen, Ingmar Bergman, Josef von Sternberg, George Cukor, and Pedro Almodóvar.

It should be noted, though, that the most famous animation studio in film history, the Disney Studios, has put women at the forefront of many of their movies: *Snow White and the Seven Dwarfs, Cinderella, Alice In Wonderland, Sleeping Beauty, Lady and the Tramp* and *Mary Poppins* during Uncle Walt's lifetime, and in later movies such as *Mulan, The Little Mermaid, Beauty and the Beast, Pocahontas, The Princess and the Frog,* etc.

Having a female character in the lead role doesn't make much difference, though, if everything else in the film is patriarchal and masculinist. So the notions of feminism, and female agency, and women's empowerment, and how women are portrayed and perceived, is problematic. It's not enough to point out that a picture has some key female characters; it's much more complicated than that.

It's important, for instance, that women are not often depicted in a very negative light in Hayao Miyazaki's cinema, as they are in so many American movies. The images of women in Miyazaki's tend to be positive and life-affirming. Some of the women in Miyazaki's movies are very strong characters: you wouldn't mess with San in *Princess Mononoke* or Nola in *Laputa: Castle In the Sky* or Yubaba in *Spirited Away.* And the young heroines of Miyazaki's movies are also tough, practical and assertive characters: Kiki, Nausicaä, Fio, Chihiro (and sometimes they might not start out wholly confident and independent, like Chihiro, but they usually end up like that: *Spirited Away* charts the journey of a young girl from insecurity, anxiety and dependence to self-confidence and independence).

Why so many female characters? One reason Hayao Miyazaki offered was that when girls do something,[64] it's kinda automatically more interesting than when boys do something:

> If a boy is walking with long strides I think nothing of it, but if a girl is walking boldly, I think she looks so full of vitality. That's because I'm a man: women might think a boy striding along looks cool. (SP, 428)

Because Hayao Miyazaki is a man: yes, it *is* that simple sometimes. Miyazaki would rather look at girls than boys, and would rather have girls as the main character than boys. Asked about his preference for female characters, Miyazaki replied that it was a complicated issue, but reduced his explanation to this: 'it's because I love women very much'.

A criticism of the depiction of female characters in Hayao Miyazaki's cinema might be that he and his writers have simply transferred male/ masculine attributes to a female character (as Hollywood movies do — consider Hollywood action movies, such as *Alien, G.I. Jane, Catwoman, Underworld, Kill Bill*, etc).

I don't think that Hayao Miyazaki's films do that, though; I don't think of Miyazaki's female characters as simply female versions of male characters. In fact, it's more that in some cases, Miyazaki's cinema doesn't make that much of gender differences. His characters don't angst about being female or male – they are too busy getting on with being themselves. There are few examples of characters voicing views such as

---

[64] Think of the scene in *Spirited Away* when Chihiro clambers down the wooden staircase outside the bathhouse, and compare it with a boy doing it. Or Chihiro facing off against No Face on her own in the painted room.

'girls shouldn't do that', or 'women don't do that'.

Hayao Miyazaki has commented a number of times on wanting to provide positive role models for young Japanese women, and *Spirited Away* was made partly to do that. It was partly a movie produced for young women, who weren't being catered for, Miyazaki thought, in movies. Certainly *shojo* characters[65] such as Nausicaä and Kiki and Fio (in *Porco Rosso*) are positive role models – they are hard-working (a vital Miyazaki characteristic), independent (also important), idealistic, optimistic, helpful, confident, warm-hearted, and (crucially) compassionate. They are characters who believe in themselves and what they are doing.

It's true they can be too idealistic (and naïve) at times, and have to adjust their hopes and dreams to fit reality; they can be irritatingly enthusiastic, and have to temper their enthusiasm; they can be headstrong, and stubborn.

But they are seldom negligent of other people's feelings; they are deferential (and remember their manners when others remind them, as Lin does to Chihiro in *Spirited Away*); they are trusting, and loyal. And, unlike too many young characters in Western animation, they are never bratty.[66] Miyazaki has also avoided overly cute depictions of young women, which are everywhere in Japanese animation: they do have the large eyes and tiny mouths of *animé* women, but they are not babes or dolls.[67] Large breasts are common in Japanese *animé*, but in Miyazaki's films they are reserved for older matriarchal figures, like Dola in *Laputa* or Yubaba in *Spirited Away*.

Hayao Miyazaki recognized that *shojo manga* (comic-

---

65 The *shojo* character is a young girl, somewhere between a child and an adult. The *shojo* is marked by a fondness for popular culture, for cute consumer goods (*Kawaii*), a wistful nostalgia, and an innocent eroticism (S. Napier, 118). Many of Hayao Miyazaki's characters are *shojo*, of course, although some critics have seen Miyazaki's young women as 'youths wearing *shojo* masks'. Cuteness is certainly a key element in Miyazaki's young female characters. It's no surprise that many of Miyazaki's *shojo* characters are linked to flight, because flying represents escape *par excellence*.
66 Hayao Miyazaki has also avoided portraying *shojo* characters as sexually objectified and 'play toys for Lolita complex guys' (SP).
67 A. Osmond, 1998.

books depicting young women) were really psychological: the real story took place in the text and the blank spaces of the page, not in the visuals. Thus, in turning a *shojo* comicbook into an animated movie the real question was: 'how much of a person's psychological state can really be represented with visuals' (SP, 101). That question is central to the animation of *Spirited Away*.

Hayao Miyazaki's female characters are at their worst when they are self-absorbed, like Chihiro at the beginning of *Spirited Away*, or Kiki when she's loses confidence in her witchy ability. When they are passive, like Clarisse in *The Castle of Cagliostro*, they conform more to stereotypes of princesses in towers who need to be rescued by dashing princes (Lupin III).

Hayao Miyazaki's women are at their best when they are brave, and kind-hearted, and compassionate, and confident in their decisions. When they trust themselves, and when they gain the trust of others. They can be just as heroic as guys, and often more heroic (Nausicaä, Kiki) – because they are the heroines, the chief characters, and no one else is going to do it if they don't. Often they have to act alone, without help or back-up, and sometimes without really knowing what they are doing.

That is Chihiro's situation: she learns early on that only she can save her parents: Haku tells her of the set-up of the bathhouse, and what she has to do, and he helps her (and other folk help her, such as Kamaji, Lin, Zeniba, etc), but, ultimately, it's Chihiro who has to do it all. And she has to draw on her resources, on her gut instinct. Haku could probably do a lot more if he really devoted himself to the task of freeing Chihiro's parents, but the scene in the elevator following the interview with Yubaba is critical in showing Chihiro (and the audience) that Haku has his own problems and duties. If it's going to get done, Chihiro realizes she will have to do it herself.

CHARACTERS: THE LOOK

In terms of compositions and figures, the films of Hayao Miyazaki feature recurring types. The children, for instance, are wonderfully energetic, laughing characters, with large eyes and enormous mouths that stretch across their whole faces when they laugh. They are squat, round body types, that bounce around a scene like basket balls.

The heroes and heroines tend to be rather intense, with the clean, pure lines of classical beauty, and the familiar features of Japanese *animé*: wide eyes (always with a couple of eye lights), tiny button noses, small, neat mouths, and fabulous, spiky, wild hair (that usually wafts in the breeze, and not only in flying or magical scenes). They are usually highly agile and dynamic, sometimes clumsy, and usually possess slender bodies like dancers.

The older men in Hayao Miyazaki's cinema run from tall, skinny, neurotic types to gruff, burly, muscular figures. Short, portly figures recur (like Marco in *Porco Rosso* or the old engineer in *Laputa: Castle In the Sky* or Jigo in *Princess Mononoke*). Some are dynamic adventurers, like Lord Yuba in *Nausicaä of the Valley of the Wind,* and some are dynamic but comic, like the Mamma Aiuto's boss in *Porco Rosso*. Miyazaki loves moustaches and beards (in films such as *Nausicaä of the Valley of the Wind,* there's no mouth at all for some of the male characters, just a giant bushy shape).

Another character type that Hayao Miyazaki has made his own is the powerful older woman, usually rather large, sometimes with a vast bosom, very big hair, and typically an enchantress. The costumes are usually skirts and dresses, with hair in traditional styles, such as buns: the crone in *Nausicaä of the Valley of the Wind,* the Witch of the Waste in *Howl's Moving Castle,* and the one that tops them all, the totally incredible, once-seen-never-forgotten Yubaba in *Spirited Away*.[68]

---

[68] Yubaba is the finest example in all cinema of the crazy, powerful matriarchs in Lewis Carroll's *Alice* books, the Duchess, the Red and the Queen of Hearts.

Few Hayao Miyazaki heroes or heroines wear jeans and Tee shirts, crop-tops or bikinis,[69] baseball caps, tattoos or piercings. Sometimes overalls or dungarees, sometimes army uniforms, and sometimes, like Pazu in *Laputa: Castle In the Sky*, a shirt and breeches. The young women tend to wear dresses or skirts (Kiki hates her dark witch's dress).[70] The costumes are dictated very much by the periods which Miyazaki and his teams like to explore, of course: the late 19th century and early 20th century, or, occasionally, more mythical eras, as in *Nausicaä of the Valley of the Wind* or *Princess Mononoke*. Chihiro in *Spirited Away* sports red shorts, sneakers and a white Tee shirt with a green stripe. Modern dress, certainly, but without logos, make-up, jewellery, etc.

As well as using women in the lead roles, Hayao Miyazaki also likes to pair up characters, so that the hero is essentially split into two. Usually, they are male and female, and are usually regarded as a couple (sometimes they actively resent being seen as a couple, like Porco with Fio in *Porco Rosso*, and sometimes they are not quite a romantic couple, like San and Ashitaka in *Princess Mononoke*). And sometimes Miyazaki likes to subvert expectations, and reverse gender roles. For instance, he makes the leader of the pirates in *Laputa: Castle In the Sky* a powerful woman, Dola. And in *Mononoke*, the tough boss of the industrial Irontown community is not a man, but a beautiful woman, Eboshi.[71]

---

[69] Ariel the mermaid in Disney's 1989 flick sports one of the more preposterous costumes for a fairy tale character.

[70] There's an erotic component to this – Hayao Miyazaki has commented that he likes skirts and dresses. And like other Japanese *animé*, the skirts and dresses tend to blow in the wind all the time.

[71] A recurring motif in Miyazaki's cinema are the pairings between older women and younger women: Kushana and Nausicaä in *Nausicaä of the Valley of the Wind*, Clarisse and Fujiko in *The Castle of Cagliostro*, Dola and Sheeta in *Laputa: Castle In the Sky*, and Gina and Fio in *Porco Rosso*. Even Chihiro and Yubaba work together in *Spirited Away*.

CHARACTERS: TYPES.

One of the strongest elements in Hayao Miyazaki's cinema, and one of the chief reasons for its enduring popularity, is surely Miyazaki's ability to create convincing and likeable heroes and heroines. These are young people (sometimes older people) that are resourceful, hard-working, brave, dignified, and creative, but also sometimes vulnerable, sometimes moody, sometimes doubting themselves and their abilities. They are not superheroes, however, though they do occasionally have some superhero traits – such as the ability to fly.

They are not petty, not greedy, not envious, not small-minded; they are generous, and kind, and helpful, and loyal. All of these positive qualities might make them insufferable and arrogant, but no, the characters in Hayao Miyazaki's films are very appealing. These are genuine people; sometimes they can be very serious, but they are also ready to laugh and fool around. At the level of characterization, the movies of Miyazaki are as convincing and persuasive as any of the great filmmakers – Charlie Chaplin, Ingmar Bergman, D.W. Griffith, Akira Kurosawa, whoever.

Most of the characters in Hayao Miyazaki's movies are white – either Japanese or European, with one or two Americans. If they're European, they tend to be French or Italian (not so many Brits or Scandinavians, for instance). 'White' meaning 'Caucasian' – but that is a visual convention of Japanese *animé*: to Japanese audiences, they would look Japanese; to Westerners they look 'white'.

DAILY RITUALS.

Another significant ingredient in the films of Hayao Miyazaki is their domesticity and everydayness: every single one of the interiors in these magical movies is a believable, lived-in space: there are pots of coffee or kettles and saucepans on the stove; there are onions or tomatoes on the table; there are bowls of milk on the floor for cats and vases of flowers on the table; there are clothes hanging up inside and outside; and there are pictures on the walls. These are places where real people live – the walls and floors are not spotlessly clean, the doors are scuffled at the bottom and around the handles, and the brickwork has cracks in it.

There is an emphasis on daily rituals, like eating, cleaning, cooking, and washing. And scenes of characters going to bed or getting up out of bed. The scenes may only be little slips of colour on a plastic animated cel, but you really can believe that Kiki is lying on her back in that big dusty room above the baker's store in *Kiki's Delivery Service,* or that Chihiro is asleep on the floor in the women's bedroom in *Spirited Away.*

STYLE

In terms of style, the animated movies of Hayao Miyazaki run from conventional cinema to sudden explosions into fantastical or heightened modes of narration. Miyazaki's use of the camera is largely traditional – classical camera moves such as slow pans to reveal an environment, or slow tilts, or slow zooms, often across verticals and horizontals.[72] Like all the best filmmakers, Miyazaki does not wave the camera around pointlessly or use self-conscious or tricky effects.[73] However, when dramatically necessary, he will employ crash zooms, or whip pans, or rapid tracking shots, or flash cuts, or extreme close-ups. In short, Miyazaki uses the camera for a dramatic

---

[72] Hayao Miyazaki's animation simulates live-action cinema, as if the animation were being filmed with a real camera, as does Japanese animation (and most Western animation) in general: that is, it includes camera movements like pans and tilts (favourite Miyazakian shots), tracking shots, zooms, dynamic backgrounds, selective focus, wide angles, and so on. Western animation (including computer animation added to live-action movies) also simulates photographic elements such as lens flare.

[73] I'm glad that Miyazaki hasn't got into speed ramping or self-conscious editing techniques (as some fans would like to see). There's so much going on in a Miyazaki movie, you don't need that look-at-me fussiness.

reason every time. He will not cut to a God's-eye-view, for instance, when having the camera at eye-level will do just as well, or better.

One of the striking aspects of Hayao Miyazaki's cinema is how often he uses movement in space, along the right angle to the screen. Traditionally, this's trickier to achieve convincingly in animation (the flattened movement from right to left or left to right is more common. Think of the 1960s Hanna and Barbera cartoons, where characters run past recycled backgrounds).

In films such as *Spirited Away, Princess Mononoke* or *Laputa: Castle In the Sky,* characters race towards the camera, or away from the camera, creating a dynamic sense of movement and composition. There's never a feeling that Hayao Miyazaki and his teams are limited in any way by the animation process. Characters move from and into all corners of the frame.[74]

In some pictures, such as *Spirited Away* and *Howl's Moving Castle,* there is an interior space where the production teams decide they are going to go all-out, to throw in every idea, every colour, every prop, every and any thing they can think of. In *Howl's Moving Castle,* this occurs in Howl's bedroom (and also the castle itself), while in *Spirited Away* it's Yubaba's apartment (and in *Arrietty,* it's the heroine's bedroom). On the visual level, the interiors are reminiscent of the highly ornate and decorative art of Symbolist painters Gustave Moreau or Odilon Redon, or the British Pre-Raphaelite artists (such as Edward Burne-Jones or John Everett Millais or James Tissot).[75]

One of the most impressive aspects of Hayao Miyazaki's cinema is invisible: the editing and pacing. Not a frame is wasted, and none of his films seem too long or slow or

---

[74] Characters walking towards the camera is one of the most difficult things to do in animation, Miyazaki said (SP, 320) – and Miyazaki's cinema is full of such scenes.

[75] For Chris Lanier, *Spirited Away* is 'one of the most visually baroque films ever made. Its look and density are so unique', recalling ancient Buddhist frescoes or Byzantine art.

padded-out. One of the beauties of animation for the viewer is that because it's so expensive and so labour-intensive, animated movies are rarely too long. Miyazaki's pictures are as exquisitely-paced as any in the history of cinema. That is a vital element of their success. Compare, for instance, with so many Hollywood films of the same period – 1980s-2000s – and you'll find movies that drag on and on, that have every dramatic highpoint s-t-r-e-t-c-h-e-d o-u-t mercilessly l---o---n---g, each plot point will be hammered home bluntly, and the films out-stay their welcome by twenty, thirty or forty minutes.

Instead of including meanderings and atmospheric incidents, the best Japanese films focus on the main theme ruthlessly, as Bruce Kawin and Gerald Mast explain:

> the great Japanese films seem to rivet every incident of the plot, every character, every visual image, and every line of dialogue to the film's central thematic question or dominant mood. (1992b, 410)

Hayao Miyazaki's movies have wonderful, enormous and spectacular endings, and that's a key reason for their success. There are quite a few major filmmakers, for instance, who had real trouble with endings (Orson Welles, Stanley Kubrick, Steven Spielberg, and Francis Coppola, for instance). But in Miyazaki's movies, the ending is fully worked out on the narrative and thematic and emotional level: that is, Miyazaki's movies don't only deliver fantastic action and thrills and stunning set-pieces and gags and stunts, they also completely convince emotionally and thematically.

Instead of happy endings, Hayao Miyazaki said it was enough for him to have the hero deal with a single issue for the moment. It might be easier to make a movie where everyone is happy because the villain has been defeated, but Miyazaki just couldn't do that (SP). 'A film should show some problem being overcome, even if it's a small one', Miyazaki remarked in 1995 (SP, 423). In *Spirited Away*, some of the problems or challenges are Chihiro's, and she overcomes them. The external (action) story is to save her parents, but the internal (emotional, psychological) story is to grow, to become less selfish, more self-confident, less anxious, more independent.

Discussing *Future Boy Conan* in 1983, Hayao Miyazaki said that he liked it when stories ended with the characters cleansed or liberated: they become, in effect, *more* child-like or innocent at the end, rather than the conventional narrative development from innocence and naïvety to maturity and knowledge. Instead of gaining something, like wisdom, or values, or morality, or a message, things drop away. So, for Miyazaki liberation is one way to go: 'I feel that viewers should feel liberated after watching cartoon films, and that the characters should also ultimately be liberated' (SP, 304).

In *Spirited Away,* that is seen literally, when Haku is freed from the tyranny of Yubaba, and Chihiro is freed from her self-doubts and insecurities. Even Yubaba, a character whom nothing on Earth could budge, learns to appreciate the possibilities of being less domineering and intolerant. (Well, maybe she doesn't learn anything: she turns away in a huff when Chihiro wins her test at the end).

THEMES

Among the themes that Hayao Miyazaki's cinema takes in are ecology, war, politics, depression, loyalty, the loss of innocence, consumerism, and creativity (C, 1). You can add animism, good vs. evil, nature, age and youth, flight, feminism, the future, technology, and machines to that list.

Animism is the most ancient form of religion or spiritual feeling, and predates all religions. E.B. Tylor famously defined animism as 'the belief in spiritual beings'. Animism is found throughout Hayao Miyazaki's cinema, and he has referred to it in his writings. A film such as *Princess Mononoke* or *My Neighbor Totoro* is a pæan to animistic sensibilities. And animism of course is a foundation of Shintoism,[76] Japan's main religion. In Miyazaki's movies, there are offerings to spirits (*kami*),[77] sacred gates (*torii*), and Shinto shrines (*jinja*).[78] There are evocations of Shintoism in *Spirited Away*.

<u>Nature and ecology</u> is such an all-pervasive theme in Hayao Miyazaki's cinema, and all of his films and his narratives relate to the natural world and protecting the natural world in some form or another.[79] And some movies, such as *Nausicaä of the Valley of the Wind* and *Mononoke Hime*, make ecological politics central to the narrative. For Miyazaki, ecological issues could not be ignored from around 1960: that was the time when it was no longer possible to ignore the wider world (SP, 107).[80]

Society isn't automatically progressive, always developing to greater and greater things. Although the utopian desire is all-powerful, and humans cannot live without it, Hayao Miyazaki reckoned there will be a time when, for example, there is no electricity: there will be power lines, but no electricity (SP, 421). Miyazaki often talks about the future, how technological societies will find resources and fuel running

---

[76] As the *Lonely Planet* guide to Japan explains: 'In Shinto there is a pantheon of gods (*kami*) who are believed to dwell in the natural world. Consisting of thousands of deities, this pantheon includes both local spirits and global gods and goddesses. Shinto gods are often enshrined in religious structures known as *jinga, jingu*, or *gu* (usually translated into English as shrine' (C. Rowthorn, 2007, 54).

[77] As well as *kami* or spirits, Hayao Miyazaki's movies – and Isao Takahata's – feature Buddhist icons, such as *jizo* statues (C. Odell, 28).

[78] Although *Nausicaä of the Valley of the Wind* contains images of a messiah, there are few overt references to Christianity in Hayao Miyazaki's cinema. Miyazaki said he was shocked when he first saw the images of Christ in Western art: 'I couldn't believe what repulsive images the artists had used to represent God. I was simply aghast; there was no way I could have regarded them as beautiful' (SP, 121). Miyazaki is not the only artist of recent times to react that way.

[79] Japanese want to be one with nature in old age, Hayao Miyazaki wondered, but Europeans want to confront nature and stare at it (SP, 146).

[80] In *Tales From Earthsea* by Ursula Le Guin, the young wizard Otter remarks: 'I look at the world, at the forests and the mountain here, the sky, and it's all right, as it should be. But we aren't. People aren't. We're wrong. We do wrong. No animal does wrong. How could they? But we can, and we do. And we never stop.' (45).

out, with over-population a major issue.

There is no absolute good or evil in Hayao Miyazaki's cinema. This is a fundamental moral perspective. Miyazaki is critical of stories and movies which end up happily – as if everyone is now going to live happily ever after because the villain is dead. No. Miyazaki much prefers ambiguity in all of his characters – including the good guys.

Hayao Miyazaki noted that Ursula Le Guin suggested that dark was more powerful than light in her *Earthsea* books (SP, 359), but not 'dark' in terms of 'evil'. One of the reasons that the bad guys in Miyazaki's cinema are ambiguous and not wholly evil is emotional: that is, it's due to Miyazaki's tendency to empathize with his characters emotionally, so he can't see them as all bad.

> I tend to proceed on an emotional basis. I can't do the work unless I have an emotional investment in it. I tend to pour myself into the characters. And when I do so, I start to empathize with the characters, to feel sorry for them. (SP, 299)

This *emotional basis* for Hayao Miyazaki's cinema is one of the reasons why his stories proceed at times illogically, but emotionally true. His narratives do not have strictly good or evil personalities, and they often take turns which seem odd or unusual. It is an intuitive approach to storytelling which is Miyazaki's own, and one of the things that makes his cinema so extraordinary – and so different from everyone else's. 'I'm not making a film; instead, it feels like the film is making me', is one of Miyazaki's mantras (SP, 110).

Hence the villains in Hayao Miyazaki's cinema are not your usual villains:

> I'm really not good at depicting the bad guys, frankly. They always wind up to be people who are at the core basically good. (SP, 303)

Only bad people, Hayao Miyazaki asserted, such as Mao Zedong, try to change history dramatically (SP, 298). If you turn a villain into an ugly bad guy, it's too easy to get rid of them, Miyazaki said in 1994: but if you make them more sympathetic, it becomes more complicated, a richer mix (SP, 413).

The idea of portraying good and evil in movies as simple polarities is anathema to Hayao Miyazaki:

> I know it's considered mainstream but I think it's rotten. This idea – that whenever something evil happens someone particular can be blamed and punished for it – is hopeless.[81]

Hayao Miyazaki has often said that he likes to make films he would like to see himself: 'I just want to make films I want to see' (SP, 306). Animated movies might help people feel more liberated, Miyazaki wondered, more refreshed, more relaxed: they might be able to suggest ways of liberating oneself from fears and anxieties.

Underlying the fantasy and spectacle of Hayao Miyazaki's cinema is plenty of unease and ambiguity – and sometimes Miyazaki consciously foregrounds that moral ambivalence and ideological uneasiness.[82] For instance, by making his villains not out-and-out baddies, like Eboshi, the boss of Irontown in *Princess Mononoke*, or making his heroes not wholly good guys, like Howl in *Howl's Moving Castle*.

In a conventional narrative, for example, such as a Western (Brothers Grimm) fairy tale, Yubaba in *Spirited Away* would be evil, and would be punished. But she is a much more ambiguous figure: thus, there is no villain in *Spirited Away*, and no evil force to be defeated. It just doesn't work like that in Miyazaki's moral universe.

Hayao Miyazaki's cinema is also not Gnostic or Manichaean: it does not believe that the world itself is tainted or

---

[81] Hayao Miyazaki, quoted in C. Winstanley, 61.
[82] 'I have inherited my old man's anarchistic feelings and his lack of concern about embracing contradictions' (SP, 209).

corrupted or evil (there are more filmmakers who promulgate Gnostic philosophies than one would think, even if they are not aware of it).

Time is a recurring concern of Hayao Miyazaki's cinema: the importance of the past, of ancestors, of earlier generations, and of the future. Read any interview by Miyazaki and he often discusses the past and the future. What the past was *really like* is a concern, and what the future is *really going to be like* is another.

The emphasis on time, on the past and the future, comes out in Hayao Miyazaki's movies in the depiction of ruins and abandoned spaces, another Miyazakian speciality, from *The Castle of Cagliostro* onwards, emphasizing a sense of history and the past. *Nausicaä of the Valley of the Wind* and *Laputa: Castle In the Sky*, for example, with their abandoned relics of earlier civilizations, offer a poignant commentary on what the past meant to the people at the time (excessive mechanization and industry), and just how much of that civilization and community has lasted.

The message is crystal clear: you might think that advanced capitalism and technological sophistication is wonderful and life-enhancing and is here to stay, but this current phase of civilization is just as transitory and ephemeral as the clouds or the wind.

Look at the opening of *Spirited Away:* within moments the family has entered an older realm, driving along the unmetalled track, with its ancient statuary and trees, leaving the city behind. Even the abandoned theme park is retreating into age and silence, and it's maybe less than ten years old! (From 2001 to the early Nineties).

Flight is of course a major, major theme, as outlined above.

Feminism and pro-women ethics and morality is a recurring theme, to the point where Hayao Miyazaki stands far ahead of almost every other comparable filmmaker (including in Japan). You have to look to arthouse filmmakers such as

Ingmar Bergman or Pedro Almodóvar to find a (male) director so keen on placing women at the centre of their stories.

<u>Growing up</u> and finding one's place in the world is a theme found in pretty much every Hayao Miyazaki movie: it is given a particularly Japanese flavour, but also of course it's a universal theme (D. Cavallaro, 8). The related themes of the strong bonds of socialization and the institutionalization of the individual are set against the importance of finding one's individuality and independence. It's about being both a complex individual and being a part of a complicated society.

Social responsibility, loyalty, hard work, respect, generosity, companionship, kindness and solidarity are explored at both the individual and the social level in Hayao Miyazaki's cinema, in a manner so deep and detailed – separating Miyazaki's cinema from nearly all animation, and certainly from the Disney and American type of animation.

In short, the level of *maturity* in the outlook of Hayao Miyazaki's cinema is very rare not only in animation, but in any kind of commercial cinema. We are moving far beyond good vs. evil and good guys versus bad guys, way beyond the Western world's simplistic duality which still pervades all of popular culture – and high culture.

<u>Youth and old age</u>, the differences of age and of generations, is both a theme and a common motif in Hayao Miyazaki's cinema (and not just because his movies are about children, and children and parents). Miyazaki likes to put characters of different ages together – often they are women: Chihiro and Yubaba in *Spirited Away*, for example, or Sheeta and Dola in *Laputa: Castle In the Sky*, or Kiki and Osono in *Kiki's Delivery Service*. And often communities rely on young people to do what they cannot do anymore: for instance, the Eboshi people in *Princess Mononoke* need Ashitaka to discover what is happening in the rest of the country.

Though <u>utopian</u> and often <u>optimistic</u>, Hayao Miyazaki's art is also carefully realistic and pragmatic. Not pessimistic, not defeatist, but certainly practical. His movies end with the recognition that there is plenty more work to be done. However, Miyazaki has also described himself as a pessimist, but said that he wouldn't force his own life-philosophy onto the audience of his movies, in particular children.[83]

It's important, Hayao Miyazaki said in 1979, to have characters that are fully fleshed out, who are 'life-affirming and have clear hopes and goals', and then make sure that the story 'develops as efficiently and simply as possible' (SP, 34). And Miyazaki stuck to this proviso: the *life-affirming* or positive aspects of his characters is vital, I think, to his cinema. Miyazaki doesn't want to give out 'messages', or lecture his audience (there are other places to do that than in an animated movie or TV show, he said), but he does want to send out positive, life-affirming views when it comes to his lead characters and their hopes and dreams.

Hayao Miyazaki would never, and has never, created an anti-hero as his main character, or featured characters who are nihilistic or even pessimistic. Miyazaki's characters might be subject to bouts of depression (like Kiki), or might be 'cursed' by the gods (like Ashitaka), but they are not pessimists or nihilists. However, they might be anarchistic, and rebellious — but usually that's part of their bid for independence and individuality.

A decent motive: in a 1988 lecture, Hayao Miyazaki descried the motives of characters in current animation: there are two: work and sex (SP, 84). Robots fight because they are robots, police pursue criminals because they are police, and so on. Nothing but the work ethic. Or it was sex. For Miyazaki, there had to be better motives than that.

Technology is a key theme in Hayao Miyazaki's cinema, in particular how human societies relate to technology, and how technology is being used to exploit the Earth's resources. There is also a fetishistic exaltation of technology in Miya-

---

[83] At the time of *Spirited Away*, Miyazaki remarked: 'In fact, I am a pessimist. But when I'm making a film, I don't want to transfer my pessimism onto children. I keep it at bay. I don't believe that adults should impose their vision of the world on children, children are very much capable of forming their own visions. There's no need to force your own visions onto them.'

zaki's movies,[84] which sometimes runs counter to the deeply critical treatment of technology.[85]

'Fan service' in Japanese animation means delivering to audiences something fetishized and glamourized: mecha (robots and machines),[86] for example, lovingly depicted, or something sexy – glimpses of underwear or parts of the body. Needles to say Hayao Miyazaki's movies contain 'fan service' – though almost always of the mecha, fetishistic kind.

War is one of Hayao Miyazaki's fascinations, and it crops up in many of his films, from *Nausicaä of the Valley of the Wind* to *Howl's Moving Castle*. 'I'm fascinated by wars and I read a lot about them' (SP, 399). And it fascinates his colleague, Isao Takahata too: Miyazaki produced the movie *Grave of the Fireflies*, which was directed by Paku-san.

War corrupts people, it corrupts their sense of ideals and justice: *pace* the war in the Balkans of the early Nineties, Hayao Miyazaki said (in 1994): 'the thing about war is that even though people may have a sense of what is just in the beginning, once you start a war that sense of justice inevitably becomes corrupted' (SP, 399).

LOVE STORIES.

There are love stories in Hayao Miyazaki's cinema, but they tend to either be youthful and idealistic romances between teenagers, or detached, wistful relationships among older characters which are not consummated. There are many tender and affectionate scenes in Miyazaki's cinema, but only

---

[84] Only filmmakers such as George Lucas rivalled Hayao Miyazaki in creating myriad forms of technology. Miyazaki's films were deeply in love with machines and technology, especially vehicles such as planes.

[85] Hayao Miyazaki liked people who looked after machines, he said, who didn't trade in their cars every year for a new one. 'I prefer people who detect a kind of animistic power in the marvel of machines' (SP, 420).

[86] One could discuss at length the significance of cyborgs and robots and hybrid lifeforms in Hayao Miyazaki's cinema, in the light of the theories of Donna Haraway or Slavoj Zizek – you know the theories: the 'return of the repressed', the undead, zombies, ghosts in the machine, animated machines, dolls, puppets, computers with souls, etc etc etc… but I'll leave that up to other writers. (See, for instance, D. Haraway's "A Manifesto For Cyborgs", and *Primate Visions* (Routledge, London, 1989), and *Simians, Cyborgs, and Women* (Routledge, London, 1991).)

a few kisses (hugs being more common).87 And no sex scenes. Instead, flying scenes or some other experience stands in for sexual desire, which's common in movies (dancing being the most obvious synecdoche for lovemaking in Hollywood cinema – think of Ginger and Fred, or Leslie and Gene). As flying is so central to Miyazaki's art, it's understandable that flying scenes should stand in for sexual expression (the flying scene with Chihiro and Haku in *Spirited Away* is exactly that, a love scene: they fly with their heads together, holding hands, and Chihiro weeps).

The typical love story in Hayao Miyazaki's cinema is between two young people; they might be ten years old (as in *Spirited Away*), or thirteen (as in *Kiki's Delivery Service*), or around that age (in *Laputa: Castle In the Sky*). And when Miyazaki did portray a 'grown-up' sexual relationship – between Gina and Marco in *Porco Rosso* – it was similarly chaste and restrained. The emotion was certainly there, but the expressions of it were demure.

It hardly needs to be said that the love stories in Hayao Miyazaki's movies are always heterosexual. And though the families he depicts might sometimes be broken, they are usually the classic configuration of mom, dad and two kids.

THE OCEAN AND WATER.

Pretty much every Hayao Miyazaki movie features the ocean, and sometimes it's such a prominent element: the sea in *Porco Rosso*, for instance, with its numerous islands, including Rosso's idyllic island retreat.88 Or the coastal town in *Kiki's Delivery Service*. Halfway thru *Spirited Away*, the bathhouse becomes surrounded by the ocean.

And just think of the numerous towns that are set beside the sea: in *Kiki's Delivery Service*, in *Porco Rosso*, in *Howl's Moving Castle*, in *Ponyo On the Cliff By the Sea*, and in *Laputa:*

---

87 Although porn and *hentai* takes up a large part of Japanese animation, much of *animé* is chaste and restrained. For instance, the first onscreen kiss in all Japanese cinema occurred as late as 1946 (G. Mast, 1992b).

88 And even when *Porco Rosso* moves inland, to Milan in Italy, there's a major sequence involving the chase and escape via a river.

Castle In the Sky (the military island).

And even those movies which don't contain the ocean – such as *My Neighbor Totoro* or *Princess Mononoke* – feature rivers or lakes or forests so big and juicy with life they are equivalents of the ocean. (*Princess Mononoke* has a large lake, the beautiful pool at the heart of the forest, and a river in flood).

And one of Hayao Miyazaki's specialities is the sunken land or town, which appeared in his first film, *The Castle of Cagliostro*, the Roman ruins underneath the lake. The sunken areas of the flying land of Laputa. The submerged forest in *Nausicaä of the Valley of the Wind*. The flooded railway line in *Spirited Away*. And the submerged Japan in *Ponyo On the Cliff By the Sea*.

In short, water is everywhere in Hayao Miyazaki's cinema, for all of the obvious reasons: it adds life and beauty to scenes, it is perfect for animation in a variety of styles, it is central to human life, and it has any symbolism you want to attach to it.

And when it comes to animating water, one of the tough challenges of animation (you could portray the history of animation techniques by studying how animators depict water), Studio Ghibli is extraordinarily accomplished.

ANIMALS.

It's impossible to miss the importance of animals in Hayao Miyazaki's cinema: a staple of animation since its earliest incarnations, animals in Miyazaki's art perform a variety of functions. The cuddly, cute sidekick is a recurring animal, just as it is in the Walt Disney canon. Miyazaki is as happy to sentimentalize animals as much as Disney or Fox or Warners or any other contemporary animation studio.

Particular specialities are cats and dogs (the dog in *Howl's Moving Castle*, and the cat Jiji in *Kiki's Delivery Service*, for instance). *Sherlock Hound* was an entire TV *animé* series of anthropomorphic dogs. Miyazaki and his animators have clearly studied cats and dogs very closely (only Mamoru Oshii among Japanimation directors rivals Miyazaki for dog-loving). Some Miyazaki and Studio Ghibli products have animals at their heart: *Ponyo On the Cliff By the Sea, Ponpoko* and *The Cat Returns*.

And there are also animals as nature spirits, fierce, independent, unmanageable, wild – dragons, Totoros, forest spirits, wolves. Animals as pets and friends: the red elk that Ashitaka rides in *Princess Mononoke*. Hayao Miyazaki's films also invent plenty of animals – the giant bugs in *Nausicaä of the Valley of the Wind,* the Forest God in *Princess Mononoke*, and of course the Totoros.

In *Spirited Away,* animals are everywhere: one of the key decisions was to stylize the workers in the bathhouse as anthropomorphized animals: men with frog heads, for instance. The stylizations are instinctive and intuitive, which is how Hayao Miyazaki likes to work: the symbolism, though obvious, is actually secondary. Thus, turning Chihiro's parents into pigs is a poetic choice, though the elements of symbolism and mythology add plenty of nuances.

Animals in *Spirited Away* are also ingredients in the many magical transformations: characters such as Yubaba and Haku, for example, have animal alter egos. And of course the gods or spirits in *Spirited Away* feature some of Hayao Miyazaki's wildest (and funniest) fantasies of animal life.

FOOD.

As all great storytellers for children know, food plays a huge part in a child's life, and Hayao Miyazaki knows this very well. There are many scenes involving food and meals in Miyazaki's cinema:

🌾 there's a humorous scene in *Ponyo On the Cliff By the Sea* where Ponyo and Sosuke eat dinner and drink honeyed tea, and the details are exquisitely realized – of children waiting patiently at a table, of being desperate to eat, of making a mess, and Ponyo's little look of disappointment when her pack of noodles comes out broken in her dish, while Sosuke's remain neatly whole.

※ in *Laputa: Castle In the Sky*, Pazu has breakfast on the go when Sheeta wakes up, and when he returns home, disheartened, halfway through the movie, he finds Dola and her boys happily eating their way through the place. Dola's gang are over the moon when Sheeta joins them – it means good food.

※ the breakfast scene in *Howl's Moving Castle*, in which Sophie cheers Markl up no end by providing a cooked breakfast.

※ Kiki delivers food on her broomstick in *Kiki's Delivery Service*.

※ in *Porco Rosso*, the pig takes a meal in Gina's hotel.

※ in *Spirited Away*, food takes on negative connotations – the monster spirit No Face wolfs down everything, and Chihiro's parents are turned into pigs when they break a fairy tale taboo, and eat without getting permission. Food is linked to inner emotions, too: Haku gives Chihiro something to eat which'll stop her literally fading away, as she cowers in fear in the early scenes. Later, Chihiro weeps as she eats.

HUMOUR.

It's reassuring for me that the films of Hayao Miyazaki and his teams aren't crude; they don't resort to fart jokes and toilet humour (like the farting warthog in *The Lion King* or the farting pirate in *Treasure Planet*). Nothing wrong with fart or piss or shit or whatever jokes, but they would certainly detract from the impact of Miyazaki's movies. Personally, I don't reckon that kind of childish goofing off in a fantasy movie helps any. Not that Miyazaki's films don't contain some grosser moments: *Spirited Away*, for instance, has a giant Stink God, and No Face is a giant black beast who vomits copiously.

CIGARETTES.

Like the films of Jean-Luc Godard, and the *film noirs* of the 1940s in La-La Land, the films of Hayao Miyazaki are very much what I call cancer films – movies which feature a lot of smoking. These days smoking in movies means a bad guy, and smoking's been banned everywhere on Earth (except for casinos in Nevada).

But the pictures of Hayao Miyazaki – and Jean-Luc Godard, François Truffaut, Howard Hawks, John Ford, etc – are movies where many characters happily smoke. In *Porco Rosso*, for instance, the lead characters light up with a regularity only matched by the young rebels in Godard's 1960s flicks. Yubaba in *Spirited Away* breathes out billows of smoke, as does the Witch of the Waste in *Howl's Moving Castle* (in the latter case, the smoke is part of the sorceress Suliman's bad magic).[89]

STYLE AND TECHNICAL ASPECTS

ACTION.

There's no doubt that a key feature of Hayao Miyazaki's cinema is fantastic action sequences. Like the filmmakers of *Akira* or the *Legend of the Overfiend* movies or *Ghost In the Shell* or other classic exponents of Japanese *animé*, Miyazaki and his teams are geniuses when it comes to staging chases, or battles between flying machines, or gun fights in enclosed spaces. It's not a question of being 'free' in animation to draw anything, or being able to do things you can't do in live-action, it's a question of imagination (and staging, and timing, and research, etc).

An action scene in a Hayao Miyazaki picture is not your usual action scene. Take the chase at the beginning of 1986's

---

[89] Maybe there's a biographical aspect to this – one can't help noticing that both Miyazaki and his producer, Toshio Suzuki, smoke, as do others on the production teams.

Laputa: Castle In the Sky: for a start, it takes place on a railroad track built from wood hundreds of feet above the ground in an incredibly deep valley surrounded by mountains. And it's a dual chase, with Muska the arch villain and his army train on one side, and Dola the formidable pirate and her pirate gang in their car on the other. In the middle are our teenage heroes, Pazu and Sheeta, and an old-timer engineer in a slow freight train. It's a summary of every (silent) movie train chase – such as Buster Keaton or the Marx Brothers (from *The General* or *Go West*). One can imagine Walt Disney loving this chase (Disney was famously a railway enthusiast).

After some incredible stunts, explosions, near-misses and the like, our heroes escape by falling into space (it's another literal cliffhanger moment). The question – how are they going to get out of this one? – is answered by the film's McGuffin, the magic crystal that Sheeta wears around her neck. Sheeta and Pazu float gently down an enormous mine shaft, and the picture moves into a quieter moment, setting the scene for the meeting with the wise old man character, the old miner.

All of this is meticulously worked out, and plays like gangbusters. Although it's tempting, action set-pieces in a Miyazaki movie don't stretch belief, in the way that Hollywood movies, not only from the last 20 years or so, so often do. Simply on the level of action-adventure, the movies of Hayao Miyazaki are spectacular, and have no superiors.

COLOUR.

One of the vital collaborators in Hayao Miyazaki's cinema is undoubtedly Michiyo Yasuda (b. 1943), the colour designer. As Miyazaki's movies are among the most exquisite in the history of cinema in terms of colour, Yasuda's contribution is immense. As well as organizing the hundreds of colours used in every Miyazaki film, Yasuda and her team have also helped to create a unique look for Miyazaki's pictures.[90] Simply, there are no other movies which look quite like these. Even amongst the 1,000s of *animé* OVAs, TV shows, cartoons, pop promos, commercials and movies produced by the Japanese animation industry, the films of Hayao Miyazaki are instantly recognizable.

LAYOUTS.

As to compositions and layouts, the films directed by Hayao Miyazaki are sumptuous to look at, with classical compositions being favoured (using the golden mean, or the horizon along the lower third, for instance). The action generally takes place within the safe area for television and video. Sometimes, however, Miyazaki and his teams will turn in a deliberately off-kilter composition, for dramatic effect. When Nausicaä explores the underworld forest in *Nausicaä of the Valley of the Wind*, for example, she is framed very low in one shot, to emphasize the majesty of the enormous trees above her.

No expense is spared on the backgrounds and layouts of Hayao Miyazaki's movies, with a level of detail that rivals and often bests Disney's 'golden age' films. It seems that every Miyazaki movie is at the level of the finest of Disney flicks from the 1937-1942 period: *Snow White and the Seven Dwarfs*, *Bambi* and *Pinocchio*.

For instance, the level of detail in *Spirited Away* is simply staggering. The richness of Yubaba's apartment, for example, is the densest up to that time in Hayao Miyazaki's cinema. When Chihiro runs down a corridor outside the bathroom, there are mirrors which reflect her three times (mirror shots are expensive to animate, but few filmmakers can resist mirrors – and some, such as Orson Welles and Jean Cocteau, made them central motifs in their work). *Spirited Away* is one

---

90 One of the favourite devices of Hayao Miyazaki's movies is to alter between light and dark, particularly within the same scene. Miyazaki's movies love to show lights being switched on or off, for example. Colour-wise, this means adding greys and blacks to colours, to take out the warmth and saturation.

of those pictures where you can freeze most of the frames and you have a superb image.

MOVEMENT.

The movement of the characters in Hayao Miyazaki's movies is deliberately naturalistic, and far away from the exaggerated motion of the Walt Disney canon. Miyazaki has commented that Disney's characters tend to move like ballet dancers or actors in a musical[91] – just too heightened, with lavish arms movements, for example, and exaggerated squash-and-stretch movements.[92] Disney's characters move as if they're performing to the upper circle in a vaudeville show, while Miyazaki's characters are far, far more subtle, and naturalistic (as if they know the camera is right there, and tone down their performances).

Hayao Miyazaki's people are recognizably based on real people, even though they are stylistically drawn. In Disney's films, the figures seem to be made of dough or balloons or some squashy, bouncy material (and that's not only in the 'golden era' movies like *Fantasia* or *Dumbo*, but in the latest movies like *Treasure Planet* or *Home On the Range*).[93]

Differences in scale is one of Hayao Miyazaki's recurring motifs, and it appears to be a key element in Japanese *anime*: so in Miyazaki's cinema there are giant robots, giant babies, and giant men. The macho guys in *Laputa: Castle In the Sky*, for instance, are much larger than real people, sporting huge barrel chests (in the fight in the street in Slug Valley, where the men pop their shirts open like Popeye or Superman). Yubaba and her son in *Spirited Away* have enormous heads, while the baby and Yubaba's bird are transformed into very small creatures.

And Hayao Miyazaki and his animators use differences in scale all the time for dramatic purposes: in some scenes, they

---

[91] Indeed, the filmmakers of Disney's *Beauty and the Beast* studied ballet dancers for the depiction of Belle.
[92] Hayao Miyazaki also acknowledged that much of Japanese animation 'suffered from over-expressionism' (SP, 79).
[93] *Home On the Range* cost $110 million to make: what a truly dull film.

will make their heroes appear small, to emphasize their vulnerability, say, or their fear, or their lessened dramatic influence. In particular, Miyazaki and his teams like to place something very large next to something very small: so the *ohmu* are enormous insects, and Nausicaä next to them is tiny; Tombo, hanging off the giant airship at the end of *Kiki's Delivery Service*, is a minuscule dot. In *Nausicaä of the Valley of the Wind* Asbel flies a small fighter, but he's able to bring down most of the Tolmekian fleet.

Yes, in Hayao Miyazaki's cinema, one person *can* make a difference: his films are stories of individuals who shift the balance of power in their worlds: Nausicaä most spectacularly, perhaps, but also Sheeta and Pazu in *Laputa: Castle In the Sky,* Sophie in *Howl's Moving Castle,* Marco in *Porco Rosso*, and on a more modest scale, Kiki in *Kiki's Delivery Service*. And in *Spirited Away,* Chihiro saves her parents, brings about shifts in the power relations in the bathhouse, helps to free Haku, and even teaches grand old dame Yubaba a lesson in humility.

THE SETTINGS.

The settings of Hayao Miyazaki's films have included: Monte Carlo and a fictional European country (Cagliostro) in *The Castle of Cagliostro;* a fantasy land in *Nausicaä of the Valley of the Wind* (which draws on Europe); another fantasy realm in *Laputa: Castle In the Sky* (which also draws on Europe, with Slug Valley being inspired by South Wales, the Rhondda Valley); a fictionalized Europe is again the setting for *Howl's Moving Castle, Porco Rosso* and *Kiki's Delivery Service;* but Japan is the setting for *My Neighbor Totoro, Ponyo On the Cliff By the Sea*, *Spirited Away* and *Princess Mononoke*.

It's ironic, perhaps, that many of Hayao Miyazaki's movies have been set in Europe, and have dealt with European history and culture, but three of Miyazaki's biggest successes, *Spirited Away, Ponyo On the Cliff By the Sea* and *Princess Mononoke*, have been very Japanese (i.e., set in

Japan, and drawing on Japanese mythology and culture). However, wherever they are set, Miyazaki's movies are very definitely *Japanese*.

They are movies made in Japan, by predominantly Japanese crews, for the Japanese film market, and financially backed by Japanese companies. But the European (specifically *Western* European) *milieu* and tropes give Hayao Miyazaki's movies a curious and fascinating cultural hybridity. And it works – Miyazaki's films never feel as if the European or Japanese elements aren't meshed at the deepest level.

And notice, too, that Hayao Miyazaki's movies are not set in America, or about America, or draw on American culture, and have only used one or two American characters.

EDITING.

One of the reasons that the films of Hayao Miyazaki are so successful is invisible: their editing, pacing and structure. Watching a Miyazaki movie, you know you are in the hands of a master, and a master storyteller. Simply put, Miyazaki and his teams (Takeshi Seyama[94] and Katsu Hisamura are his editors) know when to place action, when to slow a film down, when to insert back-story or motivations, and when to reveal elements of the plot (it's significant that Miyazaki has an editor credit on many of his movies).

It's not something you can learn from a book, this feeling for pace and timing and structure, and each picture is different, with different demands and possibilities. And there are no formulas (there are screenwriting manuals that claim to have the mechanics of scriptwriting down, but it ain't that easy).

But without this magical feeling for how time flows within a 80 or 90 minute movie, films soon become wearying and boring. A bad or disappointing movie is often one which

---

[94] As well as editing most of Miyazaki's movies, and Studio Ghibli's movies, veteran editor Takeshi Seyama has also edited *Akira, Steam-boy, Patlabor, Little Nemo*, and many TV series. Which makes Seyama the most important film editor in Japanese animation.

hasn't been edited smoothly or successfully (of course, studios and producers meddle with filmmakers' work all too often – but usually to the extent of taking out or altering individual scenes, but they don't take apart an entire movie, so the editing remains largely intact).

But all of Hayao Miyazaki's pictures swim by with such grace and ease. This filmmaker does not waste a second of precious screen time. His films don't feel rushed, or disjointed, or awkward, or jagged around the edges.

The pacing of Hayao Miyazaki's movies was something that John Lasseter at Pixar found inspiring, and applied it to films such as *Toy Story* and *A Bug's Life*: 'Miyazaki-san is a master of pacing', how he lets certain scenes breathe, and doesn't rush them: 'there are certain moments in a film you cannot rush through. It's important to allow the audience to reflect on what's happening on the screen' (SP, 13).

SOUND.

The sound of the wind is a recurring motif in Hayao Miyazaki's cinema, as it is in the cinema of Federico Fellini or Pier Paolo Pasolini.[95] In Hayao Miyazaki's films, the sound of the wind has both a practical or 'realistic' function or meaning, but also a spiritual or magical one. It is the sound of the flying scenes, of course, and it's the sound of the wind in the grass or crops, or the sound of a character's clothes in the breeze. But it is also the sound of something magical happening. As it is in traditional symbolism: the wind is the breath of the eternal, of the divine, of God… it is the Creative Word, the Word made flesh, etc.

And the sound of the wind is linked to all of those manifestations of the natural world in Hayao Miyazaki's cinema – thunder, and storms, and clouds, and rivers, and oceans, and trees, and mountains.

---

[95] The films of Fellini and Pasolini seem to use the same wind sound effect in numerous pictures – maybe there was only one wind sound effect in the library at Cinecittà.

MUSIC.

The music for most of Hayao Miyazaki's films is by Joe Hisaishi (b. 1950), and it contributes so much – especially to the emotional core of the movies: *Nausicaä of the Valley of the Wind*, *Kiki's Delivery Service*, *Laputa: Castle In the Sky*, *Porco Rosso* and *Spirited Away*. Hisaishi's score for *Spirited Away* is especially impressive. The collaboration of Miyazaki and Hisaishi is not to be under-estimated; it may not be as well-known in film circles as the partnership of, say, Alfred Hitchcock and Bernard Herrmann, or Tim Burton and Danny Elfman, but it's certainly a vital part of the success of Miyazaki's cinema.[96]

As well as Hayao Miyazaki's films, Joe Hisaishi has also scored many other Japanese movies, including *Ario*, *Sonatine*, *The Water Traveler*, *Kids Return* and *Venus Wars*. As well as film music, Hisaishi has composed electronic music, minimal music, piano music, pop music, and orchestral music.[97]

---

[96] And one should not forget that Isao Takahata has often undertaken the production of the music in Hayao Miyazaki's films, liaising with Hisaishi.
[97] Andrew Osmond has identified the emphasis on innocence as being particularly important to Joe Hisaishi's music, and also 'its sense of the magical, the holy' (2000).

ILLUSTRATIONS

Images from *Spirited Away*, and of Miyazaki's other movies.

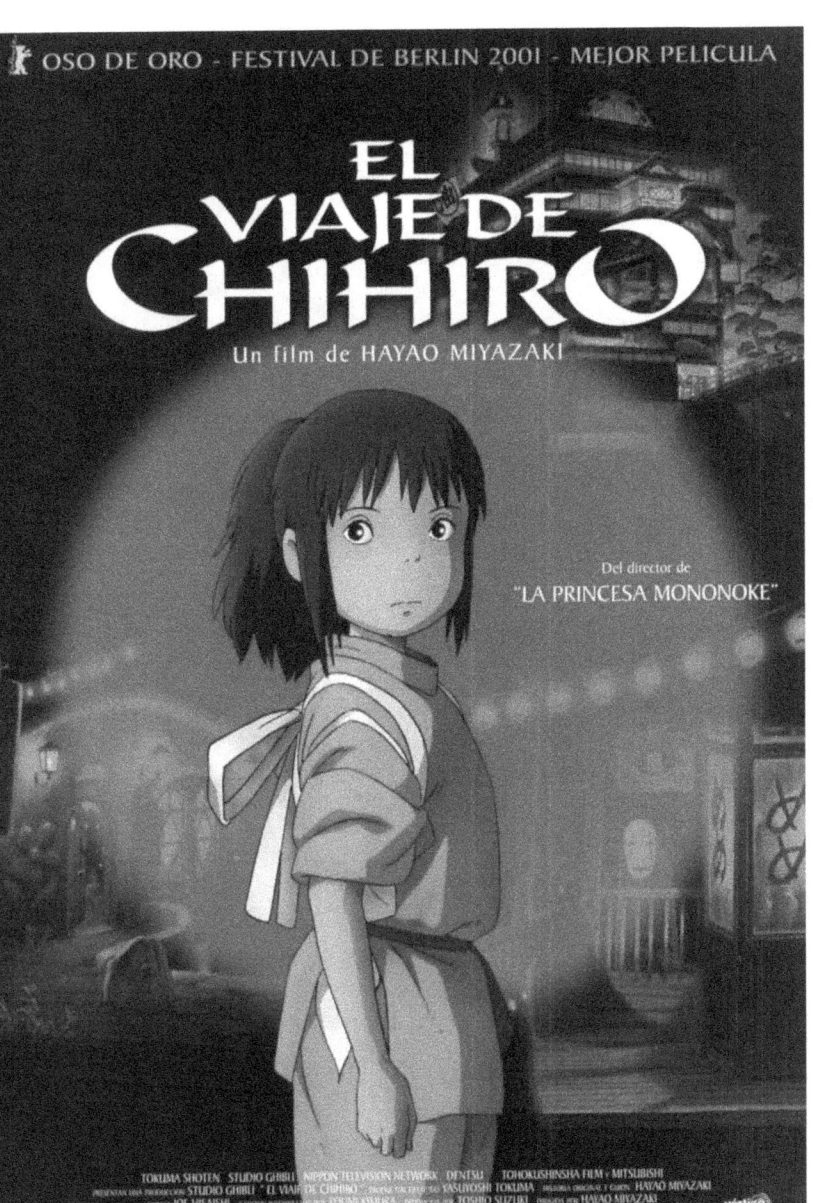

(Images from Spirited Away © Nibariki/ TNDGDDTM, 2001)

The magic begins as night falls.
Haku on the bathhouse bridge in Spirited Away,
one of numerous memorabie images in the film.

No ordinary bathhouse, it's a place where the gods themselves come to be cleansed, Miyazaki style. Some of the spirits are giant yellow chicks.

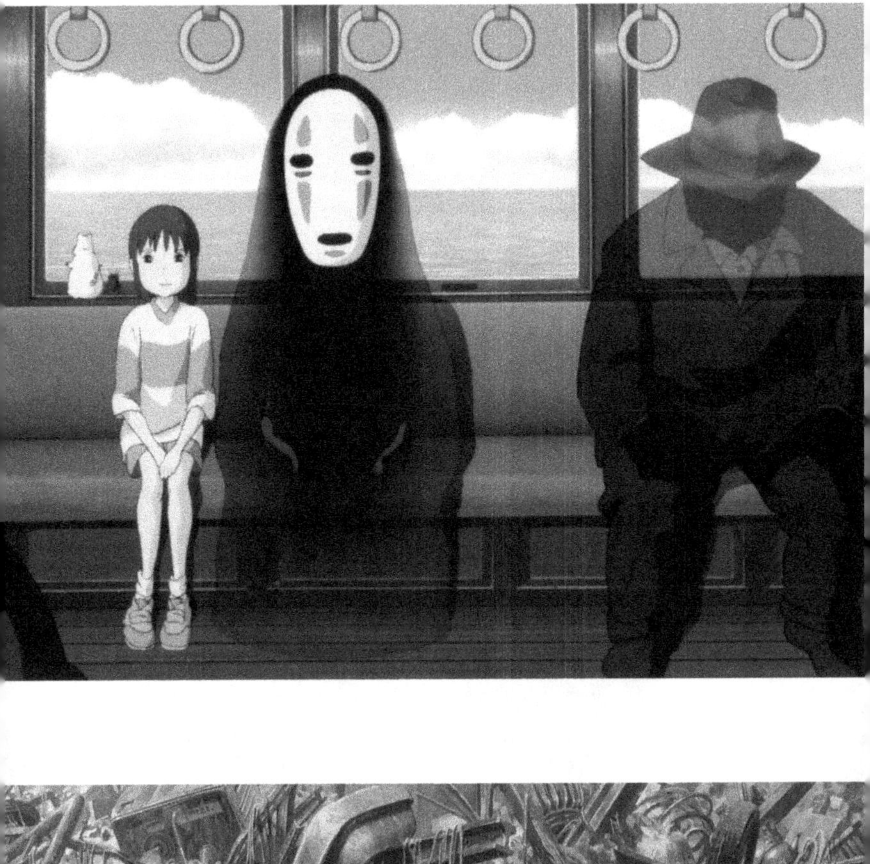

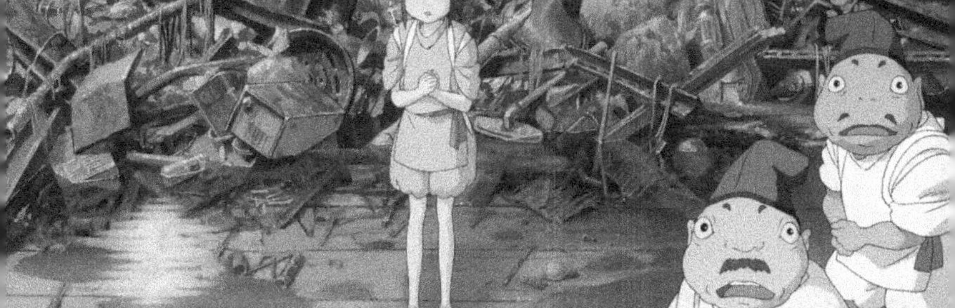
aring.com

Spirited Away is a love story, too. And if it's a Hayao Miyazaki movie, the love scene has to take place hundreds of feet in the sky.

A girl and her dragon. One of the iconic moment in Spirited Away, Chihiro and Haku re-united in the forest.

(© TMS-Kyokuichi Corporation/ Monkey Punch/ Manga Entertainment 1979)

(© Nibarki/ Tokuma Shoten/ Hakuhodo, 1984)

(© Eiko Kandono/ Nibariki/ Tokuma Shoten, 1989)

(© Nibariki/ Tokuma Shoten, 1988)

(© Nibariki/ TNDG, 1997)

(© Toho/ Walt Disney Pictures/ Wild Bunch, 2004)

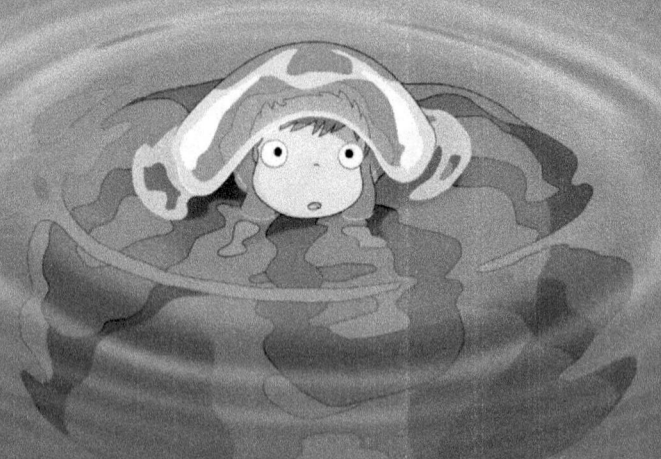

Spirited Away is partly Hayao Miyazaki's version of Alice's Adventures In Wonderland. John Tenniel's illustration of the Duchess was an influence on the witch Yubaba.

#4

SPIRITED AWAY

INTRODUCTION

Spirited Away (*Sen to Chihiro no Kamikakushi*, 2001) is without a doubt a masterpiece of cinema, and one of Hayao Miyazaki's great works. It is one of the most spectacular films of *colour* you will ever see. It's the movie that brought Hayao Miyazaki to a global audience, even more perhaps than *Princess Mononoke* (though by the time of *Spirited Away*, Miyazaki was a household name in Japan).

The voice talent for *Spirited Away* included Rumi Hiragi (Chihiro), Miyu Irono (Haku),[1] Mari Natsuki (Yubaba and Zeniba), Bunta Sugawara (Kamaji),[2] Yumi Tamai (Lin), Tatsuya Gashûin (Aogaeru), Takashi Naitô (Chihiro's father), Yasuko Sawaguchi (Chihiro's mom), Ryûnosuke Kamiki (Baby Boh),[3] Yumi Tamai (Rin), Yô Ôizumi (Bandai-gaeru), Koba Hayashi (the River God), Tsunehiko Kamijô (Chichiyaku), and Takehiko Ono (Aniyaku). The English dub,[4] produced by Kirk Wise, John

---

[1] Irono, an *anime* actor, was 13 at the time. The English dub wrongly used an older actor.
[2] The gruff, worldly-wise voice of Bunta Sugawara was also Ged in *Tales From Earthsea*. He has appeared in gangster movies (*yakuza*).
[3] Kamiki was a celebrity at 7 years-old.
[4] Subtitles were by husband and wife team Cindy and David Hewitt.

Lasseter and Donald W. Ernst at Disney[5] in 2002, included actors Daveigh Chase, Suzanne Pleshette, Jason Marsden, Susan Egan, David Ogden Stiers, Lauren Holly, Michael Chiklis, John Ratzenberger, and Jack Angel.

Art direction in *Spirited Away* was by Norubu Yoshida and Youji Takeshige. Motohiro Hatanaka was casting director. The animation directors were Kitaro Kousaka, Masashi Ando and Megumi Kagawa.[6] Music was by Joe Hisaishi (the music was produced by Kazumi Inaki and Tamaki Kojo).[7] Colour design was by Michiyo Yasuda (assisted by Kazuko Yamada). Takeshi Seyama edited the movie. Atsushi Okui was DP. Masayuki Miyagi and Atsushi Takahashi were ADs. Digital animation was by Mitsunori Katama. Sound was by Kazuhiro Hayashi and Toshiaki Abe. Takeshi Imaizumi, Tetsuya Satake and Tsukuru Takagi were sound mixers and recordists. Michihiro Ito produced sound fx. Toru Noguchi recorded the characters' sounds. Shuji Inoue's team recorded ambient sounds for *Spirited Away*, including a real bathhouse.

Part of the in-between segments and finishing work of *Spirited Away* were farmed out to an animation company in South Korea, D.R. Digital, because the production schedule of *Spirited Away* proved to be too much for Studio Ghibli. Hayao Miyazaki had visited Korea in July, 2001, to show the movie to the staff.

Other companies involved in *Spirited Away* included Anime Torotoro, Oh Production, Studio Cockpit, Studio Takuranke, Group Donguri, Nakamura Production, Gainax, Studio Kuma, Production I-G, Studio Musashi, Studio Hibari, Kiryu, Mugenkan, AIC, Liberty Ship and Mad House.

Toshio Suzuki, Yasuyoshi Tokuma, Banjiro Uemara,

---

5 A musical based on *Spirited Away*? Not impossible: the Walt Disney Company has turned many of its animations into Broadway musicals, including *The Lion King*, *The Hunchback of Notre Dame*, *Tarzan*, and *Beauty and the Beast* (plus live-action flicks like *Mary Poppins* and *High School Musical*). There are no plans to musicalize Miyazaki's movies, but I bet the idea has been considered: *My Neighbor Totoro* and *Spirited Away* are ideal for musicals.
6 There were some 40 animators working on *Spirited Away*.
7 Others in the music team included Takashi Nagai, Masayoshi Okawa, Masaki Sakjme, Shinichi Tanaka, and Futoshi Ueda.

Yuraka Narita, Koji Hoshin, Takeyoshi Matsushita, Seiichiro Ujiie and Hironori Aihara produced *Spirited Away*; and Hayao Miyazaki wrote and directed the film. The production companies, apart from Ghibli, were Nippon Television, Dentsu, Buena Vista, Tohokushinsha Film, Mitsubishi and Tokuma Shoten.

It's worth emphasizing Miyazaki's credit: the movie was *not* an adaption of a book,[8] a play, a radio series, a comicbook, a biography, a board game, a musical, a ballet, an opera, a computer game, a TV show, a remake or 're-imagining' of an earlier film, an animated version of a live-action show, a theme park ride, or a sequel: *it was an original script by Hayao Miyazaki*.[9] That in itself is pretty astounding.

> There are 1415 different shots in *Spirited Away*. When starting the project [Miyazaki explained], I had envisioned about 1200, but the film told me no, it had to be more than 1200. It's not me who makes the film. The film makes itself and I have no choice but to follow.

Moebius, Hayao Miyazaki's friend, remarked:

> when I saw *Princess Mononoke*, and even more *Spirited Away*, I was struck by the fact that I couldn't imagine a producer, any producer in the world, accepting the script.

Or put it another way: only one person in the world could've conceived, written and directed *Spirited Away*.

Spirited Away was a good experience for Hayao Miyazaki: that's important, especially for movies which mean a lot to the filmmakers.

> Creation is always a series of regrets, but *Spirited Away*

---

[8] However, one of the starting-points for *Spirited Away* was *The Mysterious Town Behind the Fog* by Sachiko Kashiwaba (1995), which depicts a girl in a strange world filled with eccentric characters.

[9] *Spirited Away* was conceived much longer, running to three hours. Miyazaki cut the movie down, simplifying it and eliminating the 'eye candy'.

was an exception. I felt really good when I was creating it. I'd always wanted to visualize a train running on the surface of the sea, and I think we came up with the scene that perfectly matches that image.

Spirited Away is a movie of many outstanding sequences, but also many modest and intimate moments.[10] There isn't an ounce of fat or waste, and nothing is too long in its 124 minute run, one of Miyazaki's longest films[11] (we've all seen pictures which seem too long even after the first ten minutes). And you can see why this production cost JPY 2.5 billion – the money is up there on the screen, in every exquisite handcrafted frame.

Spirited Away was enormously successful – like *Princess Mononoke*, it fared incredibly well at the box office in Japan. In fact, it was the biggest box office success in Japan's history, making around $250-300 million or ¥30 billion (unadjusted for inflation – only figures adjusted for inflation really make sense).[12] Its audience was in the region of 23 million, about one-sixth of people in Japan (bearing in mind that there are 127 million people living in Japan).[13]

Released on July 20, 2001 in Japan, *Spirited Away* went on to win the Best Animated Film Oscar, and numerous other awards, such as the Golden Bear in Berlin, best film at the Japanese Academy Awards, and top awards from the New York Film Critics, Los Angeles Film Critics, Annie Awards, Critics' Choice Awards, National Board of Review, Golden Satellite, Saturn, Hong Kong Film, International Children's Film, etc (of course, it shoulda won the Best Film Oscar – which went to *A Beautiful Mind* that year. *Spirited Away* beat *Ice Age* (Blue Sky/ Fox) and *Lilo and Stitch* (Disney) for the Animation Oscar).

---

10 Andrew Osmond speaks of its 'vibrant imagination, its immersive world, inimitable idiosyncrasies and eloquent fables' (2008, 106).
11 Only *Princess Mononoke* was longer, at 133 minutes.
12 The box office for *Spirited Away* was equivalent to a picture making $1 billion in the U.S.A.
13 *Spirited Away* also became the first movie to reach $200m b4 opening in the U.S.A. When it was released in America in 2002 it grossed about $10m.

Hayao Miyazaki had 'felt some hesitation about the award' (the Oscar) for *Spirited Away,* because of the U.S.A.'s actions overseas. America's war in Iraq had infuriated Miyazaki (as it had angered so many artists and thinkers around the world), and he told *Newsweek* (in 2005) that *Howl's Moving Castle* 'is profoundly affected by the war in Iraq' (O, 127)

Princess Mononoke had become the biggest grossing movie in Japan (unadjusted for inflation), the previous movie being *E.T. The Extraterrestrial* (1982).[14] *Titanic* (1997)[15] knocked off *Princess Mononoke* from the top spot,[16] but *Spirited Away* trounced *Titanic* in Japan (quite right, too!).

In 2001, the big movies globally were *Harry Potter 1, The Lord of the Rings 1, Pearl Harbor, The Mummy 2* and *Jurassic Park 3* (the usual – YAWN – sequels and franchise movies). And two other huge animated movies,[17] both digital: Disney's *Monsters, Inc* and DreamWorks' *Shrek. Monsters, Inc* and *Shrek* battled it out for the first animated movie Oscar (*Shrek* won), but had they gone up against *Spirited Away,* the competition would've stood no chance.[18] As it was, *Spirited Away* won the Oscar the following year (because *Spirited Away* was released in North America in 2002).

It's all the more remarkable when you consider who the

---

[14] *Princess Mononoke* broke *E.T.*'s record in a quarter of the time that *E.T.* had taken to make its record.
[15] Sometimes I like to believe that *Titanic* never existed – a movie that audiences went nuts over and had so much about it *not* to like.
[16] As well as *Titanic*, the big American movies of 1997 were *Jurassic Park 2* (*The Lost World*), *Men In Black, Tomorrow Never Dies, Air Force One* and *As Good As It Gets*.
[17] The other big Western animated movies of 2001 were *Atlantis, Jimmy Neutron* and *Final Fantasy,* although parts of *Evolution, Planet of the Apes, Artificial Intelligence, Dr Doolittle 2,* and *Spy Kids* were animation, like so many high budget movies.
[18] *Monsters, Inc* and *Shrek* are hugely enjoyable movies – slick, clever, flashy – but not in the same class as *Spirited Away*.

hero of *Spirited Away* is: a ten year-old girl.[19] If you asked some film studio executives or marketing experts about producing the Ultimate Money-spinning Movie, they would probably advise you to have a teenage boy (white, American) for your hero or identification figure, who teams up with preferrably some older male figure who can kick ass action-wise, plus some delicious eye candy in the form of a sexy, young starlet. *Spirited Away* has none of that. It has action in abundance, and magic, and the hint of a romance, but it breaks the rules in many other respects.

Joe Hisaishi (and his team of music editors, music supervisors, music scorers, orchestrators, recording engineers and music mixers)[20] provides a marvellous score for *Spirited Away*, one of his best, by turns haunting, sweeping, plangent, creepy, percussive and heartfelt. The music rightly provides both the emotional state of mind of the heroine, Chihiro, but also the third person views of the fantasy world of *Spirited Away*. The theme song, 'Always With Me', was by Yumi Kimura and Wakako Kaku, who had sent in the song to Studio Ghibli on spec.[21]

Spirited Away is a masterpiece of what is sometimes called 'traditional' or 'classic' cel animation. That is, drawings and ink and paint (although computers had been employed, for instance, in earlier Studio Ghibli movies, such as in *Mononoke Hime*). *Spirited Away* would be – or should be – in many critics' top ten animated films. It can happily stand beside the best of Western animation, such as the films of Walt Disney's 'golden age', and more recent movies, such as *Beauty and the Beast* or *The Lion King* (and for some will be held in higher regard). Artistically, *Spirited Away* is pretty much superior to every ink and paint animation you can think

---

[19] Many of the heroes in Hayao Miyazaki's movies are adolescents, but before teen angst and boyfriends and girlfriends: while Chihiro in *Spirited Away* is meant to be 10 years-old, and Haku a little older, and Kiki is thirteen, and Tombo about the same age, in *Kiki's Delivery Service,* and the heroes of *Laputa: Castle In the Sky* might be twelve or so, both San and Ashitaka in *Princess Mononoke* are at an age when they could get together and make love, get married, have children, etc.
[20] The music was recorded by the New Japan Philharmonic Orchestra.
[21] This would've been included in the cancelled *Rin the Chimney Painter* project.

of – and you have to search hard to find films that can match it.

The digital elements of *Spirited Away* accounted for about 100 of 1400 scenes/ shots – it included compositing, 3-D animation, object animation, texture mapping, ray tracing, morphing, ink and paint, and backgrounds. At the time of *Spirited Away,* there were three departments in Studio Ghibli using 30 work-stations: compositing, 3-D CG and ink and paint.

Computers were employed in the River God sequence, for instance, to layer levels of animation, from a painted background to shadow and reflection elements, to black-and-white gradation elements (for the water), to 3-D objects rendered by CG. *Spirited Away* was also edited on a digital Avid system.

Once again, the computer-aided animation in *Spirited Away* was cleverly integrated into the piece so that it didn't stand out as digitally-produced, but was delivered in a traditional cel animation style.

❦

Anyone can spot the increase in the *subtlety* of emotion in Hayao Miyazaki's later movies – in particular, the preponderance of conflicting feelings in the hero/ines, and the shading in those emotions. The later pieces are more emotionally complex, and contain far more conflicting motives and goals for the hero/ines than the earlier films. Which makes them satisfying in different ways. Not more 'realistic' or 'true to life', necessarily, but certainly enough to complicate the narratives even further.

And the subtlety of emotional responses also bears directly on the plots of the later Hayao Miyazaki movies, so that the hero/ines have more to consider at each move: their goals are not now simply to 'save the princess' or 'find mom'.

Spirited Away operates on so many levels. Dan Cavallaro points out some of them: 'a coming-of-age quest, a reflection on alter egos, an adult fable' and adventurous experiments in animation and technology (C, 146). There are many other layers to *Spirited Away*. For fairy tale expert Jack Zipes, *Spirited Away* depicts 'a bizarre counter-world', in which the normal world is turned upside-down:

> Everyone wants to take part in the cleansing. Nobody is purely clean. The world is chock-full of ambiguity. Deep down all the creatures want love and friendship.
> Humans, a spidery grandpa, ghosts, giant chicks, frogs, mice, and other creatures are drawn as unconventional characters that follow rituals without anything codified. The detailed depiction of the interior and exterior buildings is exquisite, and the images metamorphose before our eyes. (2011, 108)

Hayao Miyazaki insisted that although *Spirited Away* was wild fantasy, it was 'true', it was not a lie: 'I'm dealing with real issues'.[22] Audiences respond to that: the issues are real and true, they are easy to relate to: if you want to stay in Yuya (the bathhouse), you have to work. If you want to save your parents, you'll have to stay and work it out, and it won't happen instantly. There are no easy solutions.

HIGHPOINTS IN *SPIRITED AWAY*.

Among the numerous stand-out scenes in *Spirited Away* – virtually every scene – are the following:

> The first appearance of the guests at the bathhouse.
> Chihiro encountering Yubaba.
> The visit of the River God to the bathhouse.
> Chihiro climbing up to Yubaba's apartments.
> The train journey.
> Chihiro flying with Haku as a dragon.

---

[22] Quoted in S. Adilman, 2002.

WHAT IS *SPIRITED AWAY* ABOUT?

An important question to ask yourself if you are studying *Spirited Away* is: what is *Spirited Away* about? I mean, what is *Spirited Away* <u>really</u> about? Not why did the filmmakers want to make it, or how it was made, or who made it, or what the story is, or to be sidetracked by the spectacle and the visuals (though they are as distracting as in any masterpiece movie)... but to ask yourself, what is at the heart of *Spirited Away*?

Because when you've decided what the movie is really about you can assess every element in relation to that. Hayao Miyazaki has hinted at a number of levels for the movie, such as

(1) Young women coming to a city (Tokyo) or to a workplace (Ghibli) for the first time,

Or (2) the literary level of the adaption of elements from *Alice's Adventures In Wonderland*.

Spirited Away may also be about:

(3) Fnding your way in the world.

(4) It may be about growing up.

(5) It may be about 10 year-old Japanese girls.

(6) It may be about being a child dealing with adults.

(7) It may be about asserting one's identity in a world where identity is fluid and under pressure.

(8) It may be about integrating fantasy with reality.

(9) It may be about updating old folk tales for a modern audience.

(10) It may be about an economic crisis in Japan.

🍂

But *Spirited Away* is so successful as a movie, and as a work of art, and as an industrial product in a giant global industry, because it sets alight so many levels simultaneously. And some of them are very deep, thematically, psychologically, socially, and culturally.

There is a limit to the depths you can go as an audience

with many movies, and many books, or plays, or TV shows, or pop songs, or whatever. You hit the bottom pretty quick with some media products. As Hayao Miyazaki quipped of television shows, you watch a couple of minutes and you know the whole story, and everything about it, including what went on backstage.

But *Spirited Away* is a deliciously rich experience, and you can go as deep as you like with it (maybe deeper than you wanted to go initially). Hence you can see why the filmmakers spend so long on the journey to the bathhouse and the preamble to the magical world. They are leading the viewer in, gradually, gradually, slowly, slowly. They are providing moments of apparent emptiness, with not a lot happening – like the slow pans around the entrance hall, with its deliberate evocations of an empty church in dusty sunlight.[23] It's the beauty of Miyazaki's cinema that, although *Spirited Away* is a fantasy adventure with tons happening all over the place, it has many moments when it pulls back to simple and slow contemplation.

SPIRITED AWAY MANGA

Manga comics have been produced of Hayao Miyazaki's Studio Ghibli's films, just as some of Miyazaki's and Ghibli's films have been based on *manga* (such as *The Castle of Cagliostro* and *Laputa: Castle In the Sky*). For instance, as part of the merchandizing operation for *Spirited Away,* Ghibli published a *manga* version of the film, in the usual *manga* comic format of a softback book of around 160 pages. However, there was not just one book for the film, but a whole series of them.

The *Spirited Away manga* comicbook was in full colour

---

[23] Many another movie would've included summat strange or quirky in that scene, some little critter that goes 'boo!', to enhance the tension, but in *Spirited Away* the filmmakers leave the emptiness empty.

(many *manga* comics are black-and-white, apart from the cover, full colour being *a lot* more expensive to produce), and used the typical *manga* format of different sized and shaped panels (sometimes a full page of one picture, but most often five or six panels per page). The *manga* stuck very closely to the film, using the film script and dialogue. Like all novelizations or tie-in books (and all movie merchandizing, in a way), the *Spirited Away manga* was yet another means of reliving the film, or prolonging the experience of the movie.

SPIRITED AWAY AND *ALICE IN WONDERLAND*

> 'In *that* direction,' the Cat said, waving its right paw round, 'lives a Hatter: and in *that* direction,' waving the other paw, 'lives a March Hare. Visit either you like: they're both mad.'
> 'But I don't want to go among mad people,' Alice remarked.
> 'Oh, you can't help that,' said the Cat: 'we're all mad here. I'm mad. You're mad.'
> 'How do you know I'm mad?' said Alice.
> 'You must be,' said the Cat, 'or you wouldn't have come here.'

Lewis Carroll, *Alice's Adventures In Wonderland*

Wouldn't it be amazing to see Hayao Miyazaki take on *Alice's Adventures In Wonderland* and *Through the Looking Glass*? Actually, he has: it's this 2001 movie, in a way (and others). *Spirited Away* is Miyazaki's take on Lewis Carroll; it's a Japanese *Alice,* and has numerous affinities with the 1865 and 1872 books.

A gigantic industry that has grown up around *Alice's Adventures In Wonderland* and *Through the Looking Glass*: it includes 1000s of plays, school pantomimes, TV shows, cartoons, posters, books, paintings, illustrations, radio versions, fan fictions, and academic studies of the two Lewis Carroll novels. Everything in the two *Alice* books is familiar and has become part of popular culture (and not only in the West). The recent Disney movie *Alice In Wonderland* (2010) is one of the biggest productions in terms of budget and resources (and it contains acres of animation – though primarily digital).

By contrast, *Spirited Away* has a far more satisfying narrative line and emotional/ psychological development than Lewis Carroll's *Alice* books. A chief problem with all adaptions of the two *Alice* novels is the narrative structure. If you go back to the Carroll *Alice* books, you will see how the narratives move from one surreal episode to another, with few linking threads, and no sense of rising action or character development. The structure is 'curiouser and curiouser', as Alice puts it in the books. The novels don't really build up to a big climax, either, or catharsis, or pay-off, and the court case at the end of the first book is an independent section, which could appear at the beginning of the novel. It doesn't resolve many of the narrative elements of the story.

CHIHIRO

One of the inspirations for *Spirited Away* was the ten year-old daughter of a friend of Hayao Miyazaki's (and her father was an inspiration for the father in the film. One of the inspirations for the mom character was a Studio Ghibli employee). Producer Toshio Suzuki was partly responsible for persuading Miyazaki to make a movie for children, rather than the film he was planning for young people.

> What made me decide to make this film [Miyazaki remarked] was the realisation that there are no films made for that age group of ten-year old girls. It was through observing the daughter of a friend that I realised there were no films out there for her, no films that

directly spoke to her. Certainly, girls like her see films that contain characters their age, but they can't identify with them, because they are imaginary characters that don't resemble them at all.

The heroine is another of Hayao Miyazaki's very appealing characters.[24] Chihiro is very much a reluctant hero, an introverted, nervy, passive,[25] somewhat selfish, scared and spoilt child of about 10.[26] She doesn't want her life shaken up, doesn't want to move house, and misses her friends (who have given her a bunch of pink flowers and a farewell card – which handily reminds her of her name later on).

At the beginning of the film, Chihiro might grow up to be Woody Allen or James Stewart in one of their neurotic roles (Stewart in *Vertigo* – Allen in any of his movies). Chihiro is definitely not like the practical, independent young women in *Kiki's Delivery Service* or *Nausicaä of the Valley of the Wind*, or the vivacious and energetic girls like Ponyo in *Ponyo On the Cliff By the Sea* or Satsuki in *My Neighbor Totoro*. But by the end of the piece, she is.

That was the intention: Chihiro wasn't meant to have some magical power, like flying, or something she was really good at. Hayao Miyazaki and his team were keen to keep Chihiro realistic, in terms of what a young girl of ten or so would really be capable of doing (they asked themselves questions, such as, would a ten year-old girl be capable of doing this?).

Hayao Miyazaki wasn't convinced that Chihiro was appealing enough, or cute enough, although he avoids overly cute characterizations (true, Chihiro's visual characterization is not instantly appealing). By the end of production, he recognized that Chihiro wasn't dull and was charming.

Andrew Osmond (2008) draws attention to the scared,

---

[24] Miyazaki has said he tends to think about the characters and their situations for a long time b4 beginning to sketch them.

[25] Her passivity or inaction is important: she is not one of Miyazaki's all-action heroes.

[26] Miyazaki said in his statement for *Spirited Away* that it was 'for the people who used to be 10 years-old, and the people who are going to be 10 years-old'.

passive Chihiro of the earlier scenes (a characterization which was developed with animator Masashi Ando's input), and which was supplanted by the more familiar Miyazakian heroine: heroic, brave, energetic. In Osmond's reading, the more heroic Chihiro won out, as the movie was altered during production (2008, 21). Osmond even suggested that some viewers (probably adults) may have been alienated by this alteration in Chihiro's character (89). No, I don't think so at all.

Chihiro wears a white Tee shirt with a green stripe, red shorts, and sneakers. She has her bushy hair in a single bunch (when it comes to drawing women and girls, Hayao Miyazaki tends to focus on the hair above all.).[27] She is a very skinny kid, with long, spindly legs (a Hayao Miyazaki favourite form – also employed in Nausicaä in *Nausicaä of the Valley of the Wind* and Satsuki in *My Neighbor Totoro*). Chihiro has a round moon-face, with eyes set wide apart, a tiny nose (a mere fillip in profile), and large cheeks (the middle section of her face is expanded, to allow for more expressions – at times there's three inches between her mouth and her nose). In the second part of the film, Chihiro sports the uniform of the bathhouse workers: a red jacket and pants,[28] tied with a belt (and usually in bare feet – in this picture, characters are traditionally Japanese, taking their shoes and socks off indoors).

Hayao Miyazaki spoke about two of the key scenes in the film being the first one, where Chihiro is depicted in the car, afraid of the world outside, and the final scene, where she has faced the world, and is much stronger:

> But there are two scenes in *Spirited Away* that could be considered symbolic for the film. One is the first scene in the back of the car, where she is really a vulnerable little girl, and the other is the final scene, where she's full of life and has faced the whole world. Those are two portraits of Chihiro which show the development of her

---

[27] At the end of the movie, Zeniba gives Chihiro a hairband, which she's made. Miyazaki animated the moment when Chihiro puts it on (Aki Kagawa, one of the animation supervisors, recalled that some in the team thought the shot was suggestive).

[28] The costume's reminiscent of Aladdin and Sinbad.

character.

It's important for Hayao Miyazaki that Chihiro is portrayed as spoilt as well as afraid: she is a person who doesn't appreciate all of the things her parents are doing for her. Chihiro is not someone, one imagines, who has to do household chores, which she has must do in the bathhouse (and at first she's useless).

One of the views embodied in *Spirited Away* is that you already possess everything you need to do whatever it is you need to do. You don't need anything *more*. Thus, Chihiro met Haku once, but has forgotten about it: but the memory is still there, inside her (Haku says somehow he knew her name, but she doesn't know his). The sister witch Zeniba tells Chihiro: you'll have to help your parents and Haku on your own. Use what you remember about them.

THE JOURNEY TO THE BATHHOUSE

One of the delights of Hayao Miyazaki's movies are the elaborate opening credit sequences (such as in *Laputa: Castle In the Sky* or *Ponyo*). But there are no opening credits in *Spirited Away* like that: instead, after the Studio Ghibli credits and the production company credits (white lettering over pale blue, as usual), the movie goes straight into Chihiro in the car. The main title comes up over a shot of the car driving up a side road on a hill.[29]

Once again, Hayao Miyazaki and his team introduce the fantastical world of the film (the bathhouse) gradually: the movie opens with a car journey, set in the contemporary world

---

[29] Maybe it was a time issue to leave out the credits, and the filmmakers wanted to get straight into the story. It's worth noting too that *Spirited Away* is one of Miyazaki's longest movies.

(in Japan),[30] and shifts in stages to a more fantastical realm – first when the tarmac road becomes a rough track, and the city is left behind for the forest; then through the tunnel into the green fields (cue the classic Miyazakian image of clouds drifting over green hills – an image that Miyazaki has made wholly his own); across a riverbed; into the abandoned theme park; and finally to the moment when Chihiro steps onto the bridge that leads to the bathhouse. (However, the movie could've pushed Chihiro right into the midst of the bathhouse with a rapid transition: instead, it's a surprisingly gentle and elongated movement from so-called 'real life' to the heightened reality of the bathhouse. Of course, one can say that it's 'real life' which is the trance or the dream, and that the secondary world or the fantasy world is actually waking life or real life. Thus, you don't wake up *into* everyday life or real life when you return from Oz or Wonderland or the bathhouse, you really wake up when you *go to* Oz and Wonderland and the bathhouse).

The elegant transitions in the first act of *Spirited Away* (each one a threshold) lead the heroine and the audience from the 'real world' into the secondary/ fantasy world of the bathhouse one step at a time. The movie could easily have jumped from the tunnel, for instance, to the bridge across the canyon to the bathhouse. Instead, the filmmakers take the audience by the hand, just as Chihiro hangs on to her mother too tightly in the tunnel, and leads them step by step into the magical world. It is a gentler journey than suddenly thrusting the audience (and the heroine) into the magic realm.

And the *length* of the journey also serves to highlight Chihiro's emotional journey: she really is resistant to the whole idea of even entering the tunnel (she runs back towards the car, but gets scared, looks at the weird statue next to her, and joins her parents),[31] let alone crossing that eerily empty

---

[30] There are no big shots of Toyko, however, which many another filmmaker would've unable to resist: instead, the car's depicted driving along modest suburban roads, turning off to go up a hill.

[31] And how the movie exaggerates the confident walking styles of Chihiro's mom and dad enhances Chihiro's insecurities.

(though sunlit) entrance hall, or walking over the grass and the rocky stream (notice how Chihiro clambers gingerly over the rocks; notice too that her dad and mom only smell the enticing food when they have crossed the water – another example of the many fairy tale motifs in *Spirited Away* – that the river (later a lake) is the border zone of the magical world).

And Chihiro's reluctance and suspicion and fears continue up to the moment her parents turn into pigs and on and on, into the second act of the film (for a long, long time, Chihiro is having a Really Bad Day). All of that narrative work makes Chihiro's transformation into someone brave and kind-hearted and compassionate possess all the more impact (however, unlike many Miyazaki characters, Chihiro stays in the same form throughout the movie: she doesn't transform, but everyone around her does).

This *really is* a film about the journey of an individual from being selfish and self-absorbed to someone heroic and compassionate (unlike some other movies which advertize that spiritual journey, but don't deliver it). In *Spirited Away*, Chihiro is not only going to save her parents Akio and Yuko Ogino, she's also going to help Haku, *and* No Face, *and* the River God, *and* Zeniba, *and* baby Boh. *And* she even manages to teach Yubaba a lesson that bullying people isn't so good.[32] *And* she has to rediscover her name to leave the spirit world and return to her world. *Spirited Away* pulls off this remarkable narrative feat (remarkable because it's actually difficult to do convincingly), with such grace, such elegance, such skill, you can't believe it.

Someone coming to Studio Ghibli for the first time might find it labyrinthine, Hayao Miyazaki commented, referring to the bathhouse in *Spirited Away*. That was what an earlier movie, *Kiki's Delivery Service* (1989), was fundamentally about: a girl who comes to a big city, has to find a room and settle in. Kiki might be a witch, but really the movie was about 'ordinary girls who come to Tokyo from the countryside',

---
[32] In an early conception, Chihiro would've fought with Yubaba and defeated her, and then gone up against an even more powerful adversary, Zeniba.

Miyazaki said (SP, 378). Unlike Chihiro, Kiki is of course a very practical, independent girl who doesn't take long to find her way in the strange new town, and to discover a way of exploiting her talents (for flying). Chihiro takes much longer to find her feet in *Spirited Away*, but she does eventually become resourceful and determined.

In scriptwriting terms, the first act of *Spirited Away* climaxes with Chihiro's meeting with Yubaba: when the agreement is made that Chihiro will have to work at the bathhouse to save her parents, the set-up is complete. (Halfway through the first act, as usual in movie scripts, there's a turning-point: it's when Chihiro encounters her parents turned into pigs).

The scene where a family relocates to the countryside in *My Neighbor Totoro* is replayed at the beginning of *Spirited Away*, but look at the difference in Chihiro and Satsuki and Mei: for Satsuki and Mei, moving to the country is a great adventure, but Chihiro really doesn't want to move at all. She was happy where she was (it's true that Chihiro is an only child, and doesn't have a vivacious sister like Mei to play with). The older sister, Satsuki, is a sensitive, fun, protective and brave girl, and she also has that intent and somewhat serious demeanour that Kiki and Chihiro have[33] (and male characters such as Sosuke in *Ponyo On the Cliff By the Sea* or Ashitaka in *Princess Mononoke*).

And look at the *mise-en-scène* of the opening half of the first act: it's all positive, uplifting: the sky is blue, it's a warm Summer's day, there's a sunlit forest. The feelings of starting a new life in a new home (and even the adventure of leaving the tarmac road and hurtling along a forest track) ought to be fun for Chihiro. And once the family're outside the entrance foyer, the theme park is a sunlit realm of green fields and white clouds. But Chihiro resists everything.

---

[33] Hayao Miyazaki thought it would be right for Satsuki to let go just once, to cry and yell (SP, 373). Her character needed that.

OTHER CHARACTERS

Spirited Away is convincing on every level – dramatically and narratively, as well as visually or technically. All of the characters, for instance, have totally convincing personalities, from the main characters, such as Chihiro, Yubaba and Haku, to the secondary characters, such as Lin, Kamaji and the foreman. They are not types, not stereotypes, nor mere ciphers, as secondary characters (and main characters) are in too many movies. *Spirited Away* depicts a fantasy world, of course, but it's a realm where you really can believe that characters such as Yubaba the formidable, out-size witch or Kamaji the gruff, six-armed engineer exist. It's not only that if they don't exist, then they *should* exist: it's also that, within the world of this movie, they really *do* exist.

In other words, Yubaba and Kamaji and Haku and the gods are not simply fantastical creations (though they are products of an almost superhuman imagination working at its height), they are also grounded in modes of convincing behaviour, and motives, and character traits. Miyazaki and his team don't just invent amazing-looking creatures, they clothe them, give them movements, gestures and behaviour, all tailored individually. Or to re-state the obvious: *Spirited Away* is filmmaking of the highest, highest order.

As with Sophie in *Howl's Moving Castle,* Chihiro collects friends as she goes along: there is a very odd group of creatures around her which are drawn to her: there's Master Haku, the confident, prince-like boy who's also a flying dragon and ultimately revealed as nothing less than a river god. He has the blowing hair, the sleek features, and the intense stare of conventional Japananimation. There's Lin, an older sister figure and helper for Chihiro, who, though she resents having Chihiro thrust upon her by the foreman, soon gets to like her. There's No Face (*Kaonashi*),[34] an ambiguous deity that Chihiro inadvertently allows into the bathhouse (when it's raining

---
[34] Art director Yoji Takeshige was partly responsible for suggesting that No Face should form a large part of the 2nd half of *Spirited Away*.

outside, and she leaves the door open), who creates pandemonium, but it turns out that only Chihiro can really tame him – or at least, get rid of him.[35]

Two unlikely characters that become part of Chihiro's menagerie of odd companions are the baby Boh and Yubaba's bird – but they are transformed by Zeniba into a pudgy mouse and a fly, respectively.[36] Like Sophie in *Howl's Moving Castle*, Chihiro accepts these new companions, and takes them with her, carrying them on her shoulder. That acceptance is very important.

Once again, there are surrogate parental figures: with Chihiro's parents, the Oginos, out of the way (and turned into pigs, along with many other humans – straight out of Homer's *Odyssey*),[37] stand-ins present themselves: Kamaji is another of the father figures in Hayao Miyazaki's cinema: he is gruff, practical, a worker, but also kindly once you get past the crusty exterior. Design-wise, Kamaji has the requisite Miyazaki moustache and spectacles. Oh, and he happens to have six arms, which he walks on (yet his body is human), and uses to operate the boiler for the bathhouse (he turns a wheel, and mixes the water flavours from three glass jars below).[38] The arms can also extend a long way. (The more fatherly aspects of Kamaji come out, for instance, in the scene where he wakes to find Chihiro asleep on the floor of the boiler room, and picks up a mat to cover her and keep her warm. Kamaji also lies for Chihiro – he tells Lin that she's his granddaughter. Although he doesn't have any work her her, he encourages her to try Yubaba, and asks Lin to take her to see the boss. Later, Kamaji gives Chihiro the railway ticket he's been saving).

---

[35] Some critics have suggested that the relationship that No Face has with Chihiro is ambiguous to the point of having a sexual component (C, 139).

[36] The mouse and the fly are pure Miyazaki, and Miyazaki liked to animate the comedy between them himself.

[37] The theme park also has hints of *Pinocchio*, in which boys are turned into asses.

[38] And Kamaji's introduced using the German Expressionist technique of the 1920s which filmmakers have exploited for decades: out-size shadows on the wall.

The black spiders that carry the coal to the boiler, one by one, are a marvellous comic invention (cousins of the dust bunnies in *My Neighbor Totoro*),[39] and they also play a part in the plot: when one spider is squashed by the piece of coal it's carrying, Chihiro helps it. There's an aspect of labour disputes and unions here, which Hayao Miyazaki alluded to in films such as *Laputa: Castle In the Sky* – because the other spiders see Chihiro throwing the coal in the furnace, and they all want to be helped.

The lesson here, which Kamaji teaches Chihiro, is that you can't interfere with people's work unless you know what you're doing, and can handle the consequences. (And it's sweet how the spiders become Chihiro's friends too – looking after her shoes, which they hide in their cubby holes, and surrounding her as she sleeps). They also play a part in a later scene, when the little black bug inside Haku looks for somewhere to hide, and the spiders gather in their cubby holes and hiss and block its path.

Workshops of one sort or another are a recurring motif in Hayao Miyazaki's cinema – clearly evoking the animation studio (and Studio Ghibli) itself, but also the co-operative spirit. In *Spirited Away* the workers band together to help the River God, for instance, in Tatarba (Iron Town) in *Princess Mononoke*, workers mine and develop iron, and in *Porco Rosso* the workers build a plane, just like the animation team puts together a film.[40] (Kamaji can be seen as an exaggerated caricature of the filmmaker or animator – working non-stop, doing twenty things at once with his multiple limbs, and sleeping right where he works – just as Miyazaki and his co-workers have done when the deadlines approach and the work gets intense).

Lin is something of a mother figure for Chihiro, but is also like an older sister, showing Chihiro the ropes (finding

---

[39] The dust bunnies in *My Neighbor Totoro* are described as *susuwatari* or travelling soot by the grandmother.

[40] And Porco Rosso, walking around and smoking and watching the women at work, recalls the film director (and perhaps Miyazaki himself) overseeing his/ her film crew at work.

her clothes, showing her where to sleep and work). It's important that when Lin first encounters Chihiro in the boiler room, she doesn't freak out like many of her cohorts do at the sight (or smell) or a human; instead, she accepts her (though grudgingly at first).

The main surrogate maternal presence in *Spirited Away* is Yubaba – and the device of Yubaba having a twin sister (Zeniba) is another example of splitting one character into two opposing personalities.[41] Yubaba and Zeniba clearly (and vividly) embody the good mother and the bad mother. Both witches, Yubaba and Zeniba are two halves of one person. Yet Yubaba is not an evil witch: her softer side is revealed in the interview scene, when Chihiro asks for a job, and it's disclosed that Yubaba is also a mother (with a very large baby that she dotes on). As the story unfolds, it's revealed that when it comes to her baby, Yubaba is as gooey and indulgent as any mother.[42]

Chihiro cleverly manipulates Yubaba's soft spot for her baby (as Haku does too). Her baby is the only person who can really get the better of Yubaba; at the end of the piece, Boh reminds Yubaba that if she isn't nice to Chihiro, he will cry (and Yubaba only grants Chihiro permission to work in the bathhouse during a tricky time when she's trying to calm her big baby Boh down: one of the tests that Chihiro overcomes and wins at this moment is to keep persisting in demanding a job from Yubaba. If Chihiro had bottled that difficult moment, it might all be over).

As in *Howl's Moving Castle* and *Kiki's Delivery Service* and *Nausicaä of the Valley of the Wind* and other Hayao Miyazaki films, in *Spirited Away* compassion is a key theme: indeed, this is one of the elements that makes Hayao Miyazaki such a great director. It is a rare component among filmmakers, but it's one of the elements that distinguishes their

---

[41] There was an economic reason for this, too: it was simply cheaper to have the sisters look the same.
[42] But who is the father of Boh? The film doesn't depict anyone who has a relationship with Yubaba – man, she's gotta be difficult to live with!

work from run-of-the-mill directors.

Hayao Miyazaki does not lecture his audience, but he is keen to demonstrate that compassion for others is one of the most vital of all emotions. Characters such as Nausicaä and Kiki and Sosuke and Pazu have it immediately – they don't have to learn it, like Chihiro. But when it kicks in with Chihiro, her empathy with others and eagerness to help make her a noble and worthy individual.

Like Hayao Miyazaki's animations from *Nausicaä of the Valley of the Wind* and *Laputa: Castle In the Sky* onwards, *Spirited Away* teams Chihiro up with a boy of about her own age (making Haku slightly older is part of the dramatic function he has, which is to introduce Chihiro to the magical world of the bathhouse. One of Haku's functions, for instance, is simple but essential: exposition, to explain the world that Chihiro is entering). The scene in the elevator, when Haku and Chihiro are alone together, and Haku reminds her not to babble and distances himself from her, reminds Chihiro that Haku has problems of his own, that he is a separate person she hasn't known that long, and can't help her with everything (*Spirited Away* contains quite a few elevator scenes – the most amusing being when Chihiro is squashed against the wall by the enormous Raddish God. And even the Raddish God helps Chihiro in a way: he goes to the top floor with her, and she remembers to bow to him, after he's bowed to her. The bathhouse is a community when the niceties of ritual, gesture and deference are upheld, and oil social interactions. Notice how Lin has to remind Chihiro to say 'thank you' to Kamaji).

YUBABA

Spirited Away is a *tour-de-force* of animation, and for me it's the equal of any of the greatest animated films – whether that's Walt Disney's *Pinocchio* or *Bambi* or Jan Svankmajer's *Alice*. *Spirited Away* is a picture crammed with outstanding set-pieces. But not all of them are the big visual effects and action sequences. There is plenty of small-scale, intimate animation here which is equally staggering.

Yubaba[43] is a super-abundance of design, concept, animation[44] and execution.[45] She is the equal of any of the great animated characters in the history of cinema. Yubaba is a sorceress who's larger-than-life in every respect, an out-size diva of a witch with her giant grey hair in a bun, her enormous wrinkly face and bloodshot eyes,[46] her wrinkled fingers encrusted with colourful jewelled rings, her long red finger nails, her loud, raucous laugh, her piercing stare, her long hooked nose, and her genius with magic (which includes hurtling through the air, zipping up Chihiro's mouth, making objects dart about, controlling three bouncing heads, and flying as a bird – rather like Howl in *Howl's Moving Castle*, though it's not explained where Yubaba goes on her night flights). Even without her magic, Yubaba is a formidable presence, who rules over the bathhouse with a rod of iron, strikes fear into everyone around her, has a fierce temper, yet has the softest of soft spots for her giant baby.

Yubaba is the grandmother from hell, the really fearsome teacher you were always scared of, the great aunt from far away who comes to stay and makes your life a waking

---

[43] The Japanese word 'yu' means 'hot water', and 'baba' means 'old woman'.
[44] Animator Atsuko Tanaka was a principal contributor to Yubaba's animation.
[45] Supervising animator Masashi Ando said that the Queen in *Alice's Adventures In Wonderland* definitely influenced Yubaba (via John Tenniel's famous illustrations). Miyazaki acknowledged an indirect influence from Lewis Carroll. *Rin the Chimney Painter* was a production cancelled before *Spirited Away* which featured a character similar to Yubaba.
[46] Yubaba has ancestors in characters such as Ma Dola from *Castle In the Sky*. Mei in *My Neighbor Totoro* has the classic Hayao Miyazaki square face, and giant auburn bunches. With her feisty, independent attitude and loud behaviour, Mei is going to grow up into Ma Dola from *Laputa* or Yubaba in *Spirited Away*.

nightmare. And she knows how bad she is – and like a true diva, she loves it!

The interview scene in *Spirited Away* is one of the greatest in Hayao Miyazaki's cinema – and therefore one of the finest in all animated cinema. The inventiveness, the timing and pacing, the drama, the characterization, the interaction, the movement, the shapes and outlines, the backgrounds and layouts, the fusion of dialogue and motion, the props and colours, all are at the highest level of filmmaking.

You know it's going to be something special when the production design racks up to a dense level of decoration and colour – lavish and ornate European 18th century to early 20th century furnishings, with colours saturated. Shiny brass fittings; enormous painted cases; imposing wooden doors; intricately-patterned carpets and rugs.

The scene begins with Chihiro outside Yubaba's rooms, and being dragged along by magic (as if she's got a cable attached to her navel),[47] through a series of luxurious rooms and corridors (the doors flying open by magic, with each room being lit up in sequence). This was one of the scenes that was employed in the marketing of the film. It truly is a multi-million dollar scene.

The movie shows that Chihiro has already come quite a long way in the scene in Yubaba's rooms: Chihiro is terrified of Yubaba but is determined to get a job at the bathhouse (Chihiro's stubbornness, which we saw in the scenes with her parents, when she does *not* want to enter the tunnel, emerges here, but in a different manner – now she's going to stubbornly demand a job. And it's bravery, a key component of all Miyazakian heroes).

So even when Yubaba has told her *no*, Chihiro keeps asking. Even when Yubaba is trying to calm down her baby next door, and is getting angrier, Chihiro still insists. Even when faced with a truly formidable opponent, a shape-shifting sorceress, Chihiro still has the guts to demand a job! (What

---
[47] Chihiro forgets to knock first – she just tries the door – fatal in approaching a witch's dwelling.

keeps Chihiro so insistent? Presumably the motive of rescuing her parents – because Haku has told her it is the only way of saving them).

During that incredible scene, Yubaba tells Chihiro that she hadn't expected the girl to get that far; and later, Lin tells Chihiro that she got further than she expected (Lin admits that she thought that Chihiro was pretty dumb). Yubaba enjoys putting Chihiro down in the interview scene, which marks her down as a particularly spiteful character. Not truly vicious – Yubaba doesn't kill anyone in the narrative, for example – but you wouldn't want to get on the wrong side of the sorceress.

When Chihiro first encounters Yubaba, the witch is doing some administrative work – perhaps accounts – signing papers and putting money in a purse in a box. One of her first acts is to zip up Chihiro's mouth so the girl can't interrupt her: Yubaba is a prima donna who likes to hold forth, with nobody else having their say. Notice that it's Yubaba's curiosity about who helped Chihiro to get so far in the bathhouse that makes her unzip Chihiro's mouth; yet now Chihiro is free to ask for a job again.

One of Yubaba's finest moments of rage is in the scene in her office, when Haku turns up (now without Yubaba's controlling spell inside him) and tells Yubaba that she doesn't seem to be missing what she really values. Notice how Yubaba's attention turns *first* to the gold and *then* to her baby. But when she realizes that her child is gone her fury is magnificent to behold, with the steam and fire literally billowing from her nostrils.

The team of animators and crew use the Miyazakian hair to maximum effect at this point, with Yubaba's locks engulfing Haku in a torrent of writhing tendrils.[48] But the prince stands his ground. And the movie tops itself again, with Yubaba's diva-like deflation at the mention of her dreaded sister, Zeniba, and she crumples from witch-in-a-frenzy to an old, exhausted woman.

---

[48] And earlier, her hair's stuck with pieces of the green door that her baby Boh demolishes.

THE GODS

Once again in Hayao Miyazaki's cinema, there are monsters aplenty in *Spirited Away*. Here, the monsters are gods or spirits, nearly all of which are *not* traditional Japanese deities, but were invented by Miyazaki:[49] they include the enormous Raddish God (*daikon*),[50] a cross between a grey elephant and a sumo wrestler (another Totoro-type), a bunch of giant yellow Bird or Chicken Gods (*Ootori-sama*), a portly figure enclosed entirely in a large yellow cape and a little red hat, and his/ her smaller companion, *ushioni* in traditional costumes and antlers,[51] and a bunch of wild critters recalling Maurice Sendak's Wild Things. The *Kappa* are trickster water gods. Yubaba has three green bouncing heads as kind of pets, Kashira, in her office (for no explained reason). The male workers are giant frogs – well, not completely frogs (though there is a small green frog), but men with frog-like heads. Once again, these characters are instantly recognizable as Japanese men, like other creatures in Miyazaki's cinema. The women workers are equally stylized but recognizably human (they have elongated faces, for instance, and have bright clothing and resemble slugs).[52]

There are so many secondary characters, and in scenes that're so crowded, you have to watch *Spirited Away* a few times to see them all. Even the scenes which introduce the gods – arriving on the steam boat, and walking across the bridge – are so packed with animation it's impossible to take it all in. Because even in these scenes the viewpoint is wholly with Chihiro.

---

[49] The only ones that drew on Japanese traditions were the masked phantoms, the masks being at the Kasuga Shrine in Nara, by dancers.
[50] The Raddish God is *Oshira-Sama*.
[51] These are Cow Goblins or Spirits with Antlers, *Ushioni*.
[52] Some of the women are inspired by the Heian period (794-1192) – the dots above the eyes, for instance, echo the painted eyebrows of the period. There are also prostitutes in *Spirited Away* – that was unintentional, Miyazaki explained. But there is a scene where one of the bathhouse workers is leading a male figure.

THE SETTING

The presence of the natural world suffuses *Spirited Away* – the first image of the film is a big close-up of a bunch of pink flowers, which Chihiro holds in the back of the car. Fairly soon, the movie has the family entering the classic forest of fairy tales – it's announced by a tilt down shot of a giant tree, where the road becomes a stony lane. After the journey through the sunlit woods (with its statuary and little houses), *Spirited Away* makes the natural world a vital force in this story, much of which takes places indoors, in a bathhouse.[53] (The bathhouse, Yuya, is a place where eight million gods visit.)[54] Hayao Miyazaki had been thinking about a movie set in a bathhouse since he was a child. Miyazaki submitted two proposals based on a bathhouse, b4 the third one was accepted and developed into *Spirited Away*.

But the bathhouse has trees around it, is set upon a rocky outcrop, is filled with water flowing into baths and pipes, and in the second half of the narrative is surrounded by the ocean after heavy rains. None of the reverse angles of the bathhouse depict the distant suburbs of 'real life', for instance, where Chihiro is going to live, and where her school is. once the bathhouse is reached, the 'real' Japan falls away.

The abandoned theme park is a marvellous touch – it's as if we're exploring Hayao Miyazaki's fantasy films themselves, with the statues covered in moss and the partially decayed environment representing the rich history of Miyazaki's films (the squat, mossy statues emerge from the ground like fish – and sometimes they *are* fish).[55]

---

[53] Bathing in public is an ancient and familiar practice in Japan. In Tokyo in the 1960s there were 2,700 *sento* (public baths), and 18,000 or so in Japan (A. Osmond, 2008, 70).

[54] Some Japanese viewers found the bathhouse more Chinese than Japanese. It also contained Western influences (also drawing on the period when Japan was Westernized). But they recognized that it was a fantastical place, like no bathhouse that has ever existed.

[55] The Edo-Tokyo Architectural Park in Koganei, a favourite place for Hayao Miyazaki to visit, offered inspirations for the theme park. The film also drew on the Taiwanese hill-towns of Jiufen and Jinguashi.

The abandoned theme park in *Spirited Away* has forerunners in Hayao Miyazaki's cinema – such as the ruined palace, with its abandoned gardens, in *The Castle of Cagliostro* and the gardens and columns in *Laputa: Castle In the Sky*.

Yubaba's apartment is the most luxurious space in Hayao Miyazaki's cinema: it includes giant painted vases, carved balconies, chandeliers, a spotless marble bathroom, a white marble fireplace, bookcases, sideboards, lamps, a screen, paintings, and a desk which includes a telephone made out of a human skull (a wonderful Gothic touch).

There's also one of the richest rugs in movies (an intricately woven red carpet, where much of the action in the apartment takes place). So much time and attention has been lavished on Yubaba's apartment because of Yubaba's significance in the story. It functions as the villain's lair, and embodies Yubaba's power and prestige. As she tells Chihiro, her bathhouse is a classy operation.

It's one of the most opulent spaces in recent cinema (even the ceiling is carved in wood). It's as if the producers and director have told their crew: go nuts, do anything you like. But it all works, it all fits together and – like all of the spaces in Hayao Miyazaki's cinema – it convinces as a place where people could really live. It's an extravagant (and feminine) setting, of course, but it's not like many expensive sets in live-action movies, which are so obviously sets, where no one would want to live or could live. Miyazaki's cinema, for all its heightened fantasy, is always grounded in a liveable reality. Yubaba, for instance, isn't only a powerful witch and ambiguous villain, she's also a mom who goes around her apartment clearing up (you don't see Darth Vader or a *James Bond* villain picking up the cushions off the floor in a *Star Wars* or *James Bond* flick!).

Spirited Away is one of those films where you can freeze most of the frames and you have a superb image (not true of even many classic movies). Of rather, *Spirited Away* is one of those movies where you *want* to freeze a frame, because by the time of *Spirited Away,* the production team led by Hayao Miyazaki is layering their output with so many levels of detail, so many parts of the composition to look at, you really do need to the pause the flow to admire it all, or watch the movie again.

THE NURSERY

One of the more remarkable spaces, in a film jammed with fascinating places, is baby Boh's nursery at the top of the bathhouse. Its ancestor is the circular room at the top of the isolated tower in *The Castle of Cagliostro*, where Clarisse was held prisoner. In *Spirited Away*, the circular room also has celestial objects (clouds, a sun) painted on the ceiling, a rural storybook diorama around the walls, and is littered with giant cushions (all individually colourfully patterned). There's also green padding around the walls, and on the floor, a colonnade, unopened presents, a red toy car, a flying pterodactyl, soft toys, candy in boxes on a green table, a bookcase, a giant rag doll, a large bed with a mediæval canopy, etc. It's another piece of quaint Victoriana that features so often in Hayao Miyazaki's work, but here kitted out with rich patterns and hues. It's the Ultimate Victorian Nursery. (The number of toys, including the unopened gifts, are further expressions of the attention that Yubaba lavishes on her beloved baby. So much mother-love; her employees don't get it, so it all goes to baby Boh. Boh is spoilt to bits by his mom, who goes OTT with her affection).

A wonderful moment has Chihiro diving into the mound of cushions, to escape from Yubaba, a classic image of child-like behaviour. Meanwhile, the reveal of the giant baby Boh[56] who's inside the cushion mountain is beautifully timed (diving

---
[56] Boh may be a spoof of Kintaro, a Japanese hero who wore a *harakake* (a red apron) with his name on it.

into a pile of cushions has Chihiro reverting to the age of a toddler, and inside the pile she meets another kid being a kid. Only he's eight feet tall.[57]

WORK

Work is another theme in *Spirited Away* – people have to be given work to do at the bathhouse, otherwise they can't stay there.[58] So one of Chihiro's primary tasks, in the first act of *Spirited Away*, is to somehow get work. She tries first with Kamaji the engineer, but he won't give her a job to do. Eventually, she has to go to the top, to beg for a job from the boss, the witch Yubaba. And in *Spirited Away* Chihiro is depicted at work in many scenes. (In this respect, it is a kind of follow-up to *Kiki's Delivery Service*: and like that 1989 movie, the viewpoint also stays mainly with the young girl character. And it's about a young woman finding her place in a strange new environment).

Hayao Miyazaki's pictures do not stint on emphasizing the work ethic – labour is always a significant and not-to-be-ignored ingredient of the path of the hero/ine. In no way are Miyazaki's hero/ines lazy aristocrats, who loll about on couches and hammocks in the hazy afternoon sunshine, ordering servants to bring just one more cocktail. They always have to put in the basic work hours, whether that means cooking and cleaning, or walking and running and flying for miles, or digging and planting and harvesting.

To illustrate just how completely essential hard work is

---

[57] That Boh wants to stay indoors and not go outside, because of germs, might reflect Japanese youth, Andrew Osmond suggested, who prefer to stay in and indulge in the virtual reality of television, computer games and the internet (2008, 13).

[58] That labour can encourage a sense of responsibility and integrity and purpose might be lecturing and 'dreary moralism', as Andrew Osmond (2003) put it, but *Spirited Away* rises above that with its 'witty riffs on the theme'. But it's also a sly comment on advanced capitalism: that you have to work, otherwise you can't live. That is, you have to *do* something, and be seen doing something, all the time.

to the Hayao Miyazakian hero/ine, compare his movies with any similar action-adventure flicks, particularly those in the Western tradition. Few heroes in *Indiana Jones, Star Wars, Harry Potter, Lord of the Rings, The Mummy* and other movie franchises are depicted hard at work: they will feature one token scene of work (if at all), then move on to the story, to the action and adventure and explosions and chases and all the rest.[59]

Talking about hard work – Kamaji is such a devoted worker, he doesn't even have a bedroom – he simply sleeps where he works (like an animator!), in front of the boiler, where he prepares the herbal leaves for the bath water. (The unions would have something to say about that – but I guess the bathhouse, as run by dominatrix Yubaba, isn't unionized. Any workers threatening to go on strike would be vaporized).[60]

The economic down-turn in Japan (and around the world), when the Bubble Economy burst in the early Nineties, is clearly one of the elements behind the work theme, as it was with *Howl's Moving Castle*. The references to the abandoned theme park, for instance, are vivid manifestations of a boom-and-bust economy: Chihiro's father mentions that the theme parks were built in the early 1990s – not that long ago from 2001, when *Spirited Away* was released. Mr Ogino also tells Chihiro not to worry because he has money and credit cards (living on credit being another manifestation of a shaky economy).

Although the bathhouse is a community of workers (and hard workers too), the greedy aspects of capitalism soon erupt when the possibility of gaining some gold occurs.

---

[59] Jean-Luc Godard pointed out that people are seldom depicted at work in movies. And so he proceeded to show them working in movies such as *Slow Motion* (1979).
[60] Yet there a potential union dispute when Chihiro helps out the coal spiders and is dressed down by Kamaji for interferring.

LOSING THE PARENTS

It's significant that the first magical person that Chihiro meets is Haku, on the bridge (that is, someone that Chihiro comes to trust, and seems to be on her side, though he remains ambiguous). And as soon as Chihiro meets Haku, the magic begins: in short, night comes. A magical night. The music rolls in with an impressive cue; the shadows lengthen behind Haku in a time-lapse effect; he turns and blows something like white petals in the direction of the bathhouse (only later are these petals linked with Haku's dragon form); Haku tells Chihiro to run.

It's one of Hayao Miyazaki's most impressive sequences, combining a visionary imagination with emotionally convincing reactions (Chihiro in fear), and incredible action. Once again, it is the blob men, a Miyazaki staple – but they are just one element in this very complex sequence, which includes the black spirits floating around the amusement park (partially invisible), the lights coming on (strings of deep red lamps), night falling, Chihiro running away, and so many other stunning images: the illuminated steam boat,[61] for instance, sailing out of the night (the stream has become an ocean, and Chihiro runs right into it – she is literally out of her depth), with the gods on board, who materialize from floating masks as they walk onto the land, or the images of the stalls and restaurants lit up for the night (in this theme park, everything happens at night).

When Chihiro encounters her parents, now giant pigs still stuffing themselves at the food counter, it is a truly horrific image – particularly when her father slowly turns and falls to the ground. The addition of a shadowy figure behind the counter wielding a utensil like a whip adds even more horror to this already horrific scene. It's not as shocking as Chihiro seeing her parents die before her eyes, unable to help, but it is pretty distressing. Chihiro refuses to accept that

---
[61] It's wonderful that the gods arrive in a steam boat of all things. And the gold and scarlet lighting is deliberately exaggerated.

these giant pigs are her parents, and hurries away to find them.

When Akio and Yuko Ogino smell the magical scent of cooking, in classic cartoon style, it gets them into trouble: *Spirited Away* employs the fairy tale trope of the heroes breaking a taboo or prohibition. In this case, it is to eat food uninvited (as Yubaba explains to Chihiro later). Chihiro doesn't want them to do it, and hangs around outside the restaurant. She won't even take the few steps under the awning (her instincts prove right here – and most of the way through the movie). Her father says, don't worry, he's got money and a credit card (in a capitalist society, money solves all problems. Her father is all instinct, like an animal, following his nose).[62]

Hayao Miyazaki remarked on pigs:

> I think they fit very well with what I wanted to say. The behaviour of pigs is very similar to human behaviour. I really like pigs at heart, for their strengths as well as their weaknesses. We look like pigs, with our round bellies. They're close to us.

The loss of the parents is a classic fairy tale device, as well as a classic motif of films and novels. It renders the hero/ine suddenly alone, without protection, without a safety net, without help, without advice, without warmth and comfort. Now Chihiro has no mom's arm to cling onto. Many fairy tales of course begin with the parents gone by the start of the tale – as in *Cinderella* or *Snow White*, and as in Hayao Miyazaki's films, such as *Laputa: Castle In the Sky*. But to show the parents being dispatched on screen, in the foreground of the story, is a traumatic event, about as severe a trauma as you can have a child character undergo.

In *Spirited Away*, though, the parents have become pigs,

---

[62] Chihiro's dad tells her not to be afraid a number of times, such as when they enter the tunnel. Both Chihiro and her father are right: Chihiro is right to be cautious, but her father is also correct to say there is nothing to be scared of. Not really. Because although she is often afraid, Chihiro matches each obstacle and set-back.

and one of Chihiro's chief tasks (maybe her primary goal) is to break the spell, and restore her parents back to normal. To achieve that goal – which is an awesomely demanding quest for any child, and gives the film such emotional power – Chihiro also has to face many other obstacles, including looking for work and finding a place to stay.

For a while, Chihiro doesn't accept that her mom and dad have been turned into pigs right before her eyes, even though they sit at the same place at the counter in the restaurant, where she left them, and they wear the same clothes. She steps back in horror, and goes looking for her parents elsewhere in the theme park.[63]

This whole sequence is an outstanding example of animation and drama, with every stage in Chihiro's response emotionally convincing – the way she panics and runs, dodging the black blob men, the way she hurtles down the steps and ends up in a sea, the way she watches in fascination and fear at the illuminated town on the far bank, and the steam ship (and music) floating towards her. And her astonishment when she encounters Haku on the bridge, and finally the way Chihiro sits huddled by a wall, clutching her knees.

The differences between children and parents is a key theme in *Spirited Away*, embodied not only between Chihiro and her parents, but between Chihiro and the parental surrogates, such as the 'bad' and 'good' mothers, Yubaba and Zeniba, and figures such as Kamaji and older sister figure Lin.

The conflicts between youth and age are also manifested in the explorations of the present and the past: in *Spirited Away*, comparisons are offered throughout between tradition, folklore, ritual and the numerous elements of the past, and the contemporary world, with its credit cards, cars, abandoned theme parks and modern ways. Although *Spirited Away* is

---

[63] As Andrew Osmond noted, it takes something as horrific as this to shake Chihiro out of her passivity: 'In the harsh way of fairy tales, Chihiro's terrifying experience brings her to life' (2008, 63).

obviously nostalgic for the past and its values and traditions,[64] which it beautifully and sensationally evokes, it is also critical of them. Some of the old gods for example, such as No Face, are as greedy, insensitive, childish and darkly ambiguous as people in the contemporary world.

FLIGHT

No aircraft or pilots in *Spirited Away*, but there is some flying – well, quite a bit. Is there is a Hayao Miyazaki film *without* flying? The answer is: *no*. Yubaba becomes a portly flying bird and hovers over the spirit world; Haku is a white Chinese dragon, who flies in a number of scenes (Haku also grabs Chihiro on the bridge and flies with her); and the River God is also a dragon. And other characters float or fly (and there's a running gag on flight when the fly (Yubaba's transformed bird) carries Boh (the baby transformed into a mouse).

PHYSICAL ACTING

A marvellous example of modest but effective animation occurs in the scene where Chihiro creeps down the stairs leading down the outside of the bathhouse, from the bridge down to the boiler room (there is wind noise in this scene, emphasizing Chihiro's precarious position, and her fear). The film moves in very close, to show Chihiro extending those skinny legs slowly and gingerly. This is evocatively observed animation, absolutely convincing from a staging and action point-of-view. My son Jake used to be like that when we crossed wooden bridges with the slats showing a river or a

---

[64] Miyazaki recalled that some audiences in Japan wept when they saw *Spirited Away*, because it evoked a world and a landscape now vanished, from their childhoods.

road below; yeah, I'm still a little like that on a shaky wooden pier over the sea.

Spirited Away is particularly impressive in the physical acting[65] that Chihiro does throughout the film – her clumsiness, or her expressions of fear and the way she clutches her Tee shirt, or the running gag of the girl falling on her face with her ass or legs stuck in the air (she falls over a lot), or the way she creeps along walls or around doors.[66] There is some brilliant silent movie acting here – *Spirited Away* plays wonderfully without dialogue, because the animation is so extraordinarily expressive.

The scene where Chihiro dances about as she tries to stamp on the wriggling black bug that escapes from Haku's mouth is delightful, with plenty of humour (the soot sprites head it off, for instance, and there's a short ritual between Kamaji and Chihiro, to dissipate the effect of touching the worm: Chihiro makes a square with her fingers and Kamaji cuts it with his hand, saying cut! ('kitta!'). It's terrific, too, when the mouse and the fly re-enact the rite).

STYLE

The dominant colour theme for *Spirited Away* is red, and the filmmakers employed pure red paint to achieve a really dense red. Red is everywhere in *Spirited Away* – from the opening shot onwards. Gold was another hue of the movie, achieved by different yellows, adding highlights, and sometimes taking down the surrounding colours to make the gold stand out even more, as Yoji Takeshige, the art director, explained. Such rich colours – pinks, reds, oranges, pale blues, lilacs in the theme park (for an abandoned theme park, it looks amazing).

---

[65] In the stairs sequence, some of the animation was by Shinya Ohira.
[66] In the Stink God sequence, 'she trips, stumbles, bangs her head umpteen times', and is ridiculed, as Andrew Osmond pointed out (2008, 19). Yet she struggles through.

I've mentioned colour a lot in Hayao Miyazaki's cinema and in *Spirited Away*, but look at the stupendous use of *lighting*: *Spirited Away* is one of those movies that celebrates *light* all its manifestations;[67] it's a cinematographer's dream film. There is firelight, moonlight, candlelight, torchlight, dawn, dusk, night, etc.

The manipulation of viewpoint in *Spirited Away* is simply astonishing. This is the journey of a ten year-old girl, and throughout *Spirited Away* the camera angles and viewpoints emphasize that, in ways that one would expect: such as a low angle Orson Wellesian tracking shot behind Mr Ogino, when Chihiro and her folks enter the tunnel. But they also modulate it in numerous ways, sometimes adding more objective views of Chihiro, as well as looks into camera, and very rapidly moving subjective shots when Chihiro is with Haku, or when she hurtles down the exterior staircase.

THE OCEAN

The way that the bathhouse turns from being sited over a valley to something like an island, over an ocean, is enchanting (notice how the filmmakers often employ camera angles which emphasize the situation of the bathhouse over the water, rather than ones which link the bathhouse with the land). It's as if Hayao Miyazaki couldn't resist including the ocean – the sea (and rivers and lakes and streams and pools) – is one of the recurring motifs in Miyazaki's cinema. In *Ponyo*, the flood returns, and it's even more spectacular.

The ocean becomes instrumental in the later sequences in *Spirited Away*, such as the extraordinary, unforgettable train ride to Zeniba's house, and the train runs over tracks buried under a foot or so of clear water. Or the scene where

---

[67] Other movies of light might include *Persona, Close Encounters of the Third Kind, Citizen Kane, Sunrise, The Magnificent Ambersons, Days of Heaven, The Conformist* and *Women In Love*.

Lin and Sen look at the moonlight over the water on the balcony outside their rooms, eating. Or the scene where Sen encounters Haku in his white dragon form.

※

The breeze is again a magical force in *Spirited Away* – it occurs first when Chihiro and her parents stand before the tunnel entrance (actually, there was another wind moment, in the car, when Chihiro's mom opens the window). It recurs again, at the other end of the entrance building, hinting at unseen powers (like the shrines beside the road, and the squat statue at the tunnel entrance).

Hayao Miyazaki and his team employed stone deities in *Spirited Away* as mysterious presences, as guardians of forests and magical places. In a previous movie, such as *My Neighbor Totoro*, the shrines and temples included statues of foxes (the camphor tree in *Totoro* is next to a Shinto shrine, and has rice straw and paper streamers set around it).

MAGIC AND NAMES

The notion of the magical power of names is of course common in fairy tales, as is a hero having to use another name temporarily. I wonder if some of the inspiration for this in *Spirited Away* derives from the *Earthsea* fantasy novels of Ursula Le Guin. In Le Guin's peerless books, naming is the fundamental source of magic – to know the true name of a thing is to have power over it. Thus magic in the Earthsea world is about knowing true names, in an archaic language (the language dragons speak). When you utter the true name, you hold the essence of the thing. When the letters of Chihiro's name float up into Yubaba's hand, that describes the effect of having power over something, literally grasping it and controlling it.

In the *Alice* books, Lewis Carroll employed the fairy tale

motif of the magic of names, and how a name is vital to one's identity. In the wood in *Through the Looking Glass*, Alice is afraid of losing her name:

> 'I wonder what'll become of *my* name when I go in? I shouldn't like to lose it at all – because they'd have to give me another, and it would be almost certain to be an ugly name. But then the fun would be, trying to find the creature that had got my old name!' (229-230)

Naming's a recurring theme in Hayao Miyazaki's cinema: it's employed to bitterest effect in *Spirited Away*: when Chihiro surrenders her name to Yubaba she also gives up her identity and her individuality (it also crops up in *Ponyo On the Cliff By the Sea*, a remnant of the element in Hans Christian Andersen's story, when the mermaid has to give up her voice and her tail to remain on land).

The title in Japanese of *Spirited Away* – *Sen to Chihiro no Kamikakushi* – means *Sen and the Spiriting Away of Chihiro*, thus emphasizing names, and the relationship of magic to naming.

In *Spirited Away*, it pays off *twice* – not only in Chihiro reclaiming her name, but also in Chihiro remembering Haku's true name. At that point, when Chihiro tells Haku his true name, he dissolves from being a flying dragon to being a youth again (though luckily he is still able to fly). There's a back-story to the (love) relationship of Chihiro and Haku which's revealed as the film unfolds, and only pays off towards the end of the movie, when Haku flies into Chihiro's rooms. It involves Chihiro as a child falling to a river, and Haku being revealed as a river god. The movie includes images from that moment, such as in the River God sequence, but doesn't explain them until the full reveal when Chihiro rides Haku in his dragon form.

In the world of *Spirited Away*, Hayao Miyazaki explained, words have power. Chihiro has to be *very* careful about what she says in front of Yubaba. She mustn't say 'I want to go home' or 'no', because the witch would be able to throw her out. But if Chihiro tells Yubaba 'I want to work here', even the witch can't ignore that (H. Miyazaki, 2001).

Having to hold your breath to cross the bridge is a classic dare from childhood, the kind of games that children play. (But it relates to the notion of the bathhouse itself, of cleansing, and that humans have a smell that the creatures pick up on. And it even links to the back-story of Chihiro falling into a river and being saved from drowning). For Jack Zipes, *Spirited Away*, via the symbol of the bathhouse, deals with cleansing – 'cleansing of the soul, cleaning the air, exploring the genuine essence of relationships and work' (2011, 108).

THE STINK GOD SEQUENCE

The sequence continues with some remarkable images, such as the Stink God, now revealed as a River God (portrayed as an old holy man with a mask-like face), rising from water in near-silence, some striking underwater images (including Chihiro caught up in a watery fist, in a bubble of water), and a series of more abstract, magical shots. When it comes to delivering a montage of eye-popping imagery and haunting visual ideas and motifs, Hayao Miyazaki's cinema is up there with the best. And what's so impressive about Miyazaki's films is that these vivid visual effects sequences never feel like visual effects just for the sake of seeing some visual effects. The fx, rather, are integrated into the narrative, and emerge from the story. There is never the feeling that the movie's producers have attended a screening or a story reel presentation and, in between puffs on a big cigar, demanded an action sequence here, or some visual effects there.

In short, Hayao Miyazaki's movies don't let the visual effects, or effects for effects' sake, drive the story or drive the film. And that, unfortunately, is the case with some Hollywood films, particularly the blockbusters and the Summer and Christmas movies.

The Stink God sequence climaxes with the bathhouse celebrating, and even old Yubaba gives Chihiro a big hug and congratulates her on doing so well. Saké all round, everyone clapping, and the gods themselves dancing. This is Chihiro's first big task, and she passes it with flying colours.

The shot of Chihiro's co-workers gathered around her and praising her is very important – they have finally recognized her. But the angle looking up at the balcony high above, where the gods are rejoicing (with the Raddish God prominent, waving his arms), is incredibly significant: here is ten year-old Chihiro, a regular, unremarkable Japanese kid, who is now being applauded by gods! She has certainly come a long way. (It's as if everything that Chihiro encounters in *Spirited Away* is created specially *for her* – every obstacle, every life lesson, as with Alice in *Alice's Adventures In Wonderland*).

And yet, no matter how spectacular and incredible the Stink God episode is, it isn't an all-out success for Chihiro, because she still hasn't rescued her parents. Note too the shot of No-Face, an ominous presence in the background of the merry-making – the gold washed by the mud is his doing, of course.

For helping the River Spirit, Chihiro is rewarded with a small lump of medicine (or emetic).[68] This is not for use on humans (Chihiro tries a bite when she's on the balcony with Lin, and covers up the bad taste by gobbling her food). But the medicine pays off twice – Chihiro uses it on No Face when he/ she/ it is at the height of his/ her/ its rampage: it forces No Face to start vomiting (weakening the creature), so that the people he/ she/ it has swallowed tumble out.

This is another of numerous inspired action scenes in

---

[68] For the scene where Chihiro feeds Haku in his dragon the medicine, Miyazaki told his animators to visit a vet and see how a dog would react (this was filmed for the 'making of' documentary).

Spirited Away, beginning in a spectacular hall filled with heaps of half-eaten food and painted demons on the walls. Chihiro, like the clever, resourceful girls in fairy tales, leads No Face down the stairs, tiring him out, and forcing him to slow down and spew out his victims. Lin, who's handily organized a circular wooden tub to row Chihiro out to the railway track, is still wary of No Face, but Chihiro knows he is now powerless (he's only dangerous when he's inside the bathhouse, she tells Lin). It's also a wonderful touch when Lin warns No Face – when Chihiro can't hear her – that if any harm comes to Chihiro, he will have to pay for it.

※

Another stand-out sequence, where Chihiro really proves herself, is the Stink God sequence (the Stink God that is really a River God).[69] Lin and Chihiro (now called Sen) have been assigned the central bathroom by the foreman, and grudgingly begin cleaning it (naturally it is incredibly filthy, and Chihiro and Lin don't have the right materials for the job. Sounds familiar? That is what work is, the world over). *Spirited Away* is a film where the hero *works*, really *works*, doing physically tough work: Chihiro is shown scrubbing floors, cleaning bathrooms, running errands, looking after the customers, etc. Chihiro isn't a fairy tale heroine in the modern style, who sits about doing nothing and worrying about her situation. She only has a break at the end of the day, just like the other workers.

The arrival of the Stink God – another of the blobby, liquescent and monstrous creatures that are a staple of Hayao Miyazaki's cinema – is a wonderful scene; Yubaba senses its approach from afar; the arrival of the Stink God through the theme park, as lights are switched out and doors shut, might be out of a Clint Eastwood Western when the bad guys arrive in town. The way that everyone clears out of the way, and Yubaba and Chihiro stand stricken by the Stink God's overpowering stench, unable to move, is very amusing (how

---

[69] The River God is *Kawa no Kami*, arriving first in a Stink God or *Okusare-Sama* guise.

Chihiro's hair stands on end, as if she's put her fingers in an electric socket, with the reaction also running up her body to her hair. Earlier movies had similar effects, such as with Jiji in *Kiki's Delivery Service*).

Once again, Chihiro proves that she is made of strong stuff – not only does she handle the Stink God on her own, leading it to the big bath, dousing it with water, she also pulls out the thorn in its side[70] (it's not as simple as that, of course: the thorn – actually the handle of a bike – is attached to a cord and the whole bathhouse gathers round to yank out a ton of junk the Stink God's swallowed, beginning with the bicycle).[71] Yubaba flies down to orchestrate the tug o' war brandishing some fans, and everyone in the bathhouse joins in with some cheering and encouragement.

VISITING THE PIGS

Chihiro weeps in bed – all the other (young) women are asleep on the floor of the room (all with colourfully patterned eider-downs), while Chihiro lies awake and crying. The modest but emotive scene has someone entering the room unseen and unheard by anyone else. The point-of-view stays with poor little Chihiro, hugged up in her bed (it could be anyone – or any *thing* in the crazy fantasy world that Chihiro has landed herself in). The legs approaching and the offscreen voice identify the person as Haku, who offers to take Chihiro to see her parents in the following scene, at dawn.

The next scene shows Chihiro now moving through the deserted bathhouse in the early morning with calm confidence: instead of the fearful creeping down the external wooden staircase, she simply walks up it. Instead of cowering

---

[70] There are so many details in this sequence – such as Chihiro not being able to tie a decent knot around the bicycle handle, so Lin helps – Lin is also gutsy.
[71] The ecological concerns in Miyazaki's cinema are to the fore again: Haku mentions that his river has disappeared, and the River God is choked with trash.

along walls and around corners, she simply walks quietly down the stairs and along the corridors of the bathhouse. After facing up to a giant Stink God and dealing with that, there is nothing now in the bathhouse to be afraid of.

To emphasize in another way that Chihiro is moving into new emotional states, the movie showers her with flowers. Not literally – instead, it has heaps of multi-coloured flowers in the foreground of the shots where Haku takes Chihiro from the bridge where they meet through vegetation to the farm where the pigs are kept (via a travelling shot between banks of yellow and lilac flowers, presumably enhanced with computers). The flowers are so bright and colourful (recalling the Symbolist art of Odilon Redon or Vincent van Gogh), they indicate an ecstatic state. They hint that even if Chihiro isn't quite ready yet to accept her new life at the bathhouse, amongst new friends like Haku and Lin, she is going to be looked after, and all is going to be well.

Another filmmaker might have put this montage of yellows, oranges, blues and reds and Summery, flowery images towards either the beginning of the story (to show where Chihiro is coming from, a tranquil and colourful world), or at the end of the narrative (to show where she ends up, in a paradise of flowers, like a wedding or a celebration). But putting the flowers in the *middle* of the story acts like a foreshadowing of things to come, but also like the film is embracing Chihiro at this point, like a hug from the picture itself, to reassure her that things are going to turn out well.

Another word for it is genius filmmaking.

This sequence is all about Chihiro dealing with her parents and their transformed state: it's moving the way that Chihiro tells her parents that she will save them – but it's done by having Chihiro yell at them in panic, as if she can't believe what she's saying, so she has to blurt it out, then run off. The roles have been reversed, and it's too much for Chihiro to take in, and too much for her to deal with.

Haku sensitively acknowledges this in the following

scene, where, acting like an older brother, he crouches down beside Chihiro (next to more flowers), and offers her some food, which he says he has put a spell on, to give her energy. The spell is actually a cathartic one, designed to release Chihiro's repressed emotions about her parents and her situation: as she eats the bread, over-large grey tears spring from her eyes, like something out of *Alice's Adventures In Wonderland*. She weeps (this was animated by Miyazaki himself).

This is strikingly emotional material for something that is simply ink and paint animation. Very few animated movies have achieved this kind of subtle and sensitive emotion.

And note too that this intimate moment between the two young people (significantly outside the realm (and power) of the bathhouse itself), is where Haku explains about the notion of naming, and how Yubaba controls people by stealing their names.[72] And this's also the moment when the earlier relationship of Haku and Chihiro is indicated, when Haku tells Chihiro that he has always known her name, since they met. And when Haku also tells Chihiro that he doesn't know his own name, and has been searching for it for years, it is another point at which Chihiro can help to save Haku – she is going to remember his real name later on in the story.

Pigs of course have all sorts of negative connotations, some political and ideological – satirical cartoons of the Nazis, or Josef Stalin and KGB officers, for instance, sometimes portray them as pigs. The greedy capitalist in America and Europe is routinely caricatured as a pig (usually in top hat and tails, smoking a cigar). In the negative view, pigs snuffle around at ground level, live in their own waste, etc.[73]

In traditional symbolism, the pig or swine connotes gluttony, greed (as in *Spirited Away*), anger, lust and dirt, as well as fertility and prosperity. The Goddess of ancient times

---
[72] She magically lifts up the characters (*kanji*) from the contract that Chihiro signs into her palm. Chihiro's name is 'Ogino Chihiro', but is renamed 'Sen', comprising a single *kanji*.

[73] The pig-man was intended to embody some of Miyazaki's ideas about humanity – about humans being foolish, not divine.

was linked to the sow, with lunar and sky symbolism. In Buddhism, the pig represents ignorance and greed. In Celtic mythology, the pig is one of the symbols of the Celtic Goddess Cerridwen. In Christianity, pigs are associated with gluttony and sensuality, and Satan. In Greek mythology, pigs were sacrificed to Ceres and Demeter as fertility goddesses. The sow was sacred to Zeus, who was suckled by a sow. And so on.

For Hayao Miyazaki, the pig isn't wholly negative. Miyazaki said he had wanted to have a film with a pig in the lead role (which became *Porco Rosso*) for many years (there are pig motifs at his studio, and he has the nickname pig). In *Porco Rosso*, the pig caricature fits in with the notion of the main character as a middle-aged man[74] who has become disillusioned with life, who has let go of his dreams and ideals, who is no longer the dashing hero of youth.

Hayao Miyazaki explored the more negative connotations of pigs in *Spirited Away*, when Chihiro's parents are turned into pigs (along with other humans who've strayed into the abandoned theme park and eaten the magical food, or eaten without permission).

GIVING WITHOUT RECEIVING

Chihiro never accepts anything that No Face offers her: she is always courteous with her/ him/ it, and bows to her/ him/ it (she learns that good manners help in an institution like the bathhouse), but she doesn't take his gold, or the herbal water formulas. That's another classic fairy tale device – kindness without reward, giving without expecting something in return (this new Chihiro would do well meeting the old woman at the well in a fairy tale, the woman's who really a witch or fairy, who tests people to see if they are kind enough to give her

---

[74] Marco in *Porco Rosso* has a pig's head – it's very much a humanized version of a pig, rather like the frog men in *Spirited Away*.

some water. But the old Chihiro would've likely scampered away in fear).

No Face's form of exchange is in terms of material objects which she/ he/ it thinks Chihiro wants. And when Lin encourages Chihiro to get some of the gold that No Face's handing out to everybody, Chihiro instead goes to look for Haku. That underlines once again Chihiro's higher level of being, if you like, her higher calling, her more noble nature: while most people in the bathhouse think of nothing else but receiving some gold from No Face (they all hold boxes in anticipation), work being forgotten for the moment, Chihiro is on a mission to find (and help) Haku, her friend. Friendship above gold (and also choosing Haku above hanging out with the crowd).

And that is demonstrated dramatically in the big scene where the foreman dances before No Face, with the workers lined up on each side, and Chihiro stumbles into the throng. In her rush to find Haku, she ends up in the middle of the corridor, facing No Face. Her simple refusal of his offer of gold makes public Chihiro's nobility and integrity; but no one else can see it. The workers see a silly human that they resent being there, who's stupid enough to refuse gold when it's offered for free (they are stuck inside the fairy tale, and don't realize that no one offers gold for free without some complication attached to it).

When Chihiro returns to the pig pen (in a dream), carrying the medicine that the River Spirit gave her, she is confronted by a horde of pigs, and can't tell them apart. A horrific shot pans across the angry, grunting pigs' faces, their little black eyes staring into the camera (the image's replayed during Chihiro's final test, when she has to choose which pigs are her parents. Hence the dream acts as foreshadowing, but also prompts the audience into Chihiro's anxieties; also, it reminds the viewers of Chihiro's central dilemma: to save her parents: that's why she's living through the difficult experiences at the bathhouse. And it demonstrates that, when she has the chance to save her parents with the medicine, there might be so many animals she won't be able to tell which ones are her parents).

THE NO FACE SEQUENCE

The 2001 film places Chihiro on her own with a very simple dramatic move: it has Chihiro wake up in the workers' bedroom after everyone else has left. When she goes out onto the balcony, she sees the chimney already smoking, and the rain's created an ocean below. The tranquillity of the balcony scene contrasts with the noise and chaos of the following scenes in the kitchens and halls, as the entire bathhouse cooks like crazy for No Face.

At this point, the No Face sequence is a fantasy of greed, gluttony and power: No Face (still wearing the ancient white spirit mask) is now a grotesque black beast with a giant mouth, hurling bowls of food down its throat. Food for gold: the workers bring along dishes, plates, trays and barrels of food hoping for gold in exchange. You don't need your Karl Marx or Sigmund Freud *For Dummies* to see what's going on here – this is a material-money-gold-shit and oral-anal fantasy gone crazy. It's the community stuck at one level of experience without being able to move into other levels.

Rice, sides of ham, fish, pancake rolls, mounds of whole chickens, apples, tomatoes, even a pig's head: the bathhouse workers offer No Face everything they've got, completely forgetting themselves (and what they'll eat later on). They go nuts, yelling at No Face, holding up trays piled high with food. Only Chihiro seems to keep her head in this situation: after meeting Lin on the stairs, who encourages her to join in the fun of begging No Face for gold, she excuses herself, and goes back to the balcony.

Notice how Yubaba is absent from the frenzied No Face gluttony scenes (at first): she has to be, because she'd sense what was going on. But Yubaba finds it difficult to match the powers of the gods when they're in full flight: the River Spirit and No Face are both powerful gods, and Haku too, in his dragon guise, is a formidable opponent.

SAVING HAKU AND THE ACTION CLIMAX

When Chihiro is up on the balcony in *Spirited Away*, at first bored, leaning her head on her hands on the balustrade, the extraordinary sequence with Haku the dragon unfolds at a lightning pace. It's one of those action scenes involving flight and pursuit that Hayao Miyazaki and Studio Ghibli do so well (this sort of scene is a staple of Japanese *animé*, of course).

The animation is at the upper limits of what is achievable in this sequence, with action so brilliantly presented it is breathtaking. Once again, there are some remarkable details – the dragon-point-of-view shot zooming up the wall of the bathhouse, for example, as Chihiro leans over to watch Haku. The pursuit by thousands of white paper figures, which slam into the screen as Chihiro closes it. The deep shadow in the room. And the addition of Haku trailing *a lot* of blood (as with *Princess Mononoke*, the sudden appearance of so much blood in a family, 'PG' animated movie is startling. Presumably this amount of *human* blood would mean a higher classification, but *dragon's* blood's a different matter).[75]

But the clue to this incredible sequence is *Chihiro's reaction*: she doesn't run a mile witnessing a full-grown dragon flailing about in her bedroom, spewing buckets of blood. It's not what happens here so much as how the

---
[75] In Britain, the British Board of Film Classification rated *Spirited Away* 'PG'. Usually Miyazaki's movies are given 'G' ratings (*Princess Mononoke* is by far the bloodiest of Miyazaki's films). Presumably *Spirited Away* was allotted a 'PG' due to the scariness of some of the scenes (such as those with No-Face, or the copious blood when Haku's hurt).

characters react to it. At the beginning of the film, such a sight would've freaked Chihiro out (this was a girl spooked by an over-grown statue, for instance).[76] But now she's alarmed, yet full of sympathy for Haku. And she wants to help him. Indeed, so strong is Chihiro's response to Haku's predicament, that she is going to stop at nothing to help him. Her desire now drives the whole of the rest of the movie, up until she returns from Zeniba's cottage, to save her parents from eternal pig-life.

In screenwriting manuals, the advice for your hero/ine towards the end of a movie is to pile on the obstacles. S/he can't just reach the villain's hide-out like getting on a bus and being delivered to the villain in one piece, as calm and unruffled as a trip to the mall. No, the hero has to struggle through underwater tunnels, or leap over abysses, or fight twenty ninjas.

In *Spirited Away*, the obstacles that stand in the way of Chihiro's consuming desire to help Haku include running through the chaotic assembly surrounding No Face. Of course Chihiro can't take the elevator, that would be too easy, and she can't simply slip by No Face and the foreman, either (a nice touch has the bathhouse workers gathered around in lines, holding cardboard boxes in which they hope to collect the gold No Face's handing out).

The moment when Chihiro refuses the gold that No Face offers, in front of the whole gathering, illustrates just how far along she has travelled in her spiritual and emotional journey. Even with the two handfuls of gold that No Face offers her right in front of her face, Chihiro shakes her head, and leaves in a hurry. The gold goes everywhere, causing a mass panic as the workers dive for it.

The route up to the top floor of the bathhouse now has Chihiro in full action hero mode: the sequence is a mirror of the earlier one in which Chihiro gingerly clambered down the wooden steps one by one. In the second scene where Chihiro

---

[76] But Japanese audiences would probably have seen the statue as benign (A. Osmond, 2008, 57).

clambers outside the building, she is brave, resolved to get to Haku at whatever cost. So she slides down a corrugated iron roof, finding the only way across to a steel ladder that leads upwards is along a pipe. Chihiro's determination here is winning – the way she pulls up her pants and tightens her sleeves, preparing to run along the pipe (which breaks away from the building).[77]

True to scriptwriting manual form, the obstacles are heaped on poor Chihiro relentlessly at this point in the movie: not only does she have to climb a ladder hundreds of feet above the sea, she has to avoid Yubaba, who's in her bird form, flying nearby. And then she reaches a locked window, which won't budge, even when Chihiro turns and heaves against it. *Obstacle, obstacle, obstacle* – but here the little paper figure which stuck to her plays a role, slipping through the gap in the window, and opening it.

Once Chihiro has made it all the way up the outside of the bathhouse, and into Yubaba's apartment at considerable peril, once again it isn't simply a case of rushing over to Haku to save him. The filmmakers keep piling on the set-backs for little Chihiro. She's landed in an elegant bathroom; she hurries down a mirrored corridor (featuring triple reflections), and into baby Boh's spectacular rumpus room (another alternative career for Hayao Miyazaki and his art directors would be interior design and decoration).

When Chihiro enters Boh's nursery, she is at the heart of Yubaba's realm, and Yubaba is her chief opponent – it's the witch who has kept Chihiro's ma and pa under a spell. So it's another cliché of scriptwriting to have Yubaba approach at that very moment. Having Chihiro dive into the pile of cushions is a terrific touch – it's exactly the kind of thing a kid might do. So when Yubaba enters the room (clearing up as she goes along – Yubaba never stops being a mother), the suspense intensifies (although the viewer might think that Chihiro would be able to handle Yubaba a little better now,

---

[77] The animation wasn't exciting enough for Miyazaki, and he asked for revisions (A. Osmond, 2008, 90).

after all she's been through).

Like the masters of suspense such as Alfred Hitchcock or D.W. Griffith, Hayao Miyazaki and his filmmaking team twist up the tension even more when Yubaba starts pulling aside cushions to reveal... a giant baby. That is both unexpected and expected (the baby who lives in that nursery has to be out-size), but it's also a classic reveal (and a slight lessening of suspense), when Chihiro isn't found out yet.

When Yubaba eventually leaves, after pacifying her baby (and turning the room into its nighttime setting), the filmmakers add another two more twists for Chihiro: not only can baby Boh talk at a higher age than expected, he's able to exploit Chihiro in his own way, when he grabs her arm and bends it until Chihiro promises to do what he says. This kid must learn fast – not only does he have a big pair of lungs, he can also manipulate people to do what he wants (of course, he has the best teacher for psychological power games in his mom, Yubaba). But Chihiro is a quick thinker, too, and brandishes her bloody palm at Boh (cleverly exploiting his phobias).

But even when Chihiro manages to wrest herself free of the giant baby, and rush into Yubaba's office, there is yet another obstacle – the three green heads, which bounce around Haku, and seem to want to push him into the hole that's next to the fireplace. And yet another one – Yubaba's bird screeches into the room, attacking Chihiro as she kneels beside Haku, cradling his head.

And another obstacle, in the form of baby Boh, who stomps across the room, demanding attention. The appearance of Zeniba in Yubaba's top floor apartment at this precise moment is a stunning turn in the story. A touch of pure genius, in terms of storytelling – how she chooses to reveal herself in the midst of this noisy, chaotic scene. One can imagine Zeniba really enjoying herself, seeing how far she will let things go before revealing herself.

And how Zeniba gets there is equally imaginative: she is the single paper cut-out figure that attaches itself to Chihiro's back (the filmmakers play with this paper cut-out, having it slide around Chihiro's head to avoid being seen. At some points, it seems that Zeniba might be guiding Chihiro, but Chihiro is also learning fast how to move quickly when she needs to).

As soon as Zeniba appears, she takes complete control of the situation – she turns Boh into a mouse; Yubaba's bird into a fly; and the three heads into Boh. While this is entertaining and exciting enough, there is also a few pages of dialogue and exposition peppered through the scene[78] (Zeniba explains being the twin sister of Yubaba, for example). Before the situation can develop further, there's a stunning close to the scene, when Haku recovers enough to crush the slip of paper that represented Zeniba's spirit form, and she splits into two.

The escape from Yubaba's apartment is another of Hayao Miyazaki's eye-popping action sequences, as Haku and Chihiro topple into the hole by the fire, which leads down to the dungeons (of course, where else do trapdoors lead in the villain's stronghold?). It's also a call-back to Miyazaki's first film as director, *The Castle of Cagliostro,* where trapdoors to dungeons were used not once but three or four times. And when Haku and Chihiro fall close to the bottom of the shaft, there's a group of black spectres, like trapped souls (recalling the victims in many a dungeon, and making a change from the usual skeletons – how times have we seen skeletons in dungeons? Yes, but that's what *all* humans become, sooner or later).

For plenty of filmmakers, this action sequence would be enough, a rescue and escape, and would not be the place for a flashback. Yet Hayao Miyazaki is quirky enough to insert a flashback right here, right in the midst of a scene of his heroine falling to her doom. The flashback is to the time when Chihiro fell into the River Kohaku, and Haku, in his River God form, saved her.

Spirited Away uses match cuts and rapid dissolves to

---

[78] For Andrew Osmond, this dramatic twist and the new characters in the narrative were clumsily rendered, but the scene was certainly unexpected (2008, 93).

indicate the continuity between the present day and Chihiro remembering what happened to her as a child. We are in Chihiro's mindscreen now, and one of the signature images of *Spirited Away* – and of Miyazaki's cinema – occurs here: Chihiro staring into the camera, eyes wide open, her hair blowing in the air but also as if under water. Behind her are green fronds, and in front Haku's turquoise hair on his spine. (The scene with the River God earlier has a similar image which foreshadows this scene – as if the River Gods communicate with each other. And when it leaves the bathhouse, the River God trails across the sky as a dragon, as Haku had done).

THE TRAIN JOURNEY

The journey to Zeniba's house is one of the most enchanting scenes in all of Hayao Miyazaki's cinema.[79] The filmmakers restore a train journey to its rightful place as a wonderful experience – wondrous, but also mysterious, and also wistful, and even melancholy. The long shots are as beautiful as one could ask for, as the train rolls across the ocean on the railroad tracks underneath water, with skies going slowly into twilight and night. These are exquisite images, worthy of framing and putting on the wall, each one.

But pretty imagery is not the whole picture: the *sound* is mesmerizing, too, with the train rattling along the tracks, and the sound of water swishing. And Joe Hisaishi provides a delicate piano and string piece which enhances the wistful mood. And there are other elements, too: such as the mouse (the baby) and the fly (Yubaba's bird) hopping up and down at the window and, most mysterious of all, the other travellers. These are silent and enigmatic figures, shadowy (and, un-

---

[79] For some, the journey evoked Kenji Miyazawa's 1934 novella *Night On the Galactic Railway*. In it, the souls of the dead are taken along the river of the Milky Way.

usually, in Hayao Miyazaki's cinema, most seem to be black). They are clad in 1930s or 1940s clothes, and have a weary, sad air about them.

Where they are going, when they descend from the train, isn't explained, nor why the station contains what appears to be an entrance to a subway; maybe this part of the fantasy world connects to a metropolis like New York City or Tokyo. There's a whole other story evoked in this sequence – the movie could suddenly sidetrack and follow some of those exhausted, gloomy people. (Needless to say, a formulaic approach to scripting from a major Western film studio would certainly ditch those characters and images; they come from someplace else, they don't connect to the primary narrative, they have only a tenuous thematic link to the main themes, and, crucially, they are not 'explained' by the movie).

For Hayao Miyazaki, the railroad journey was the end of the movie: 'what for me constitutes the end of the film, is the scene in which Chihiro takes the train all by herself. That's where the film ends for me'. The train ride was about the experience of the ride itself, Miyazaki explained, when you take a journey by yourself for the first time, not the landscape through which the train passes.

It's one of those train journeys to the end of the line, where everyone else gets off, and our heroes stay on the train (actually, it's the not final station). But by the time Chihiro and No Face and the others alight, at Swamp Bottom, it is full night. No surprise that as well as the pools of the swamp, there is a forest here – a witch's house simply *must* be situated in a wood.

These scenes could be excised from the film without losing any important narrative information, what scriptwriters call a 'lift' – it is simply a journey from the bathhouse to Zeniba's house in a forest.[80] But what this sequence does, among other things, is to give the audience a breather from the action and rapidity and intensity of some of the previous

---

[80] The group of four odd characters travelling to see a witch recalls *The Wizard of Oz* for Andrew Osmond (2008, 100).

scenes. A moment of calm and peace after so much action.

It's true that Hayao Miyazaki and his team allow this train ride to last far longer than it would in an American or European animated movie, but that is also the beauty of it: at this point in an American film, and particularly a family adventure film or a fantasy film, no producer or distributor would want the piece to slow down this much, or for this long. But Miyazaki and his team have said, no, we're not going to rush here, we are not going to have only one long shot of the train and the sky and the ocean, and a couple of images inside the train, we are going to turn it into a major sequence all on its own. (If there was fight over this sequence, Miyazaki clearly won).

In Zeniba's cottage the furnishings are old-fashioned (19th century) but not mediæval;[81] it really is like visiting a grandmother (Zeniba asks Chihiro to call her 'granny'; Yubaba balks when Chihiro calls her 'granny' at the climax). There's tea, and cake, and cookies on the table (regular food, after the crazy food of the bathhouse).

LOVE STORY

Spirited Away is a love story, but a most unusual one: it involves a spoilt, nervous, modern Japanese girl of ten and a mysterious boy a little older who also happens to be a River God, with the alternate form of a flying white dragon (and he's under the influence of two witches). Haku is rightly the person that Chihiro first meets at the abandoned theme park.

In the latter part of the film, Chihiro now has two quests – apart from the main one of breaking the spell her parents are under, she also wants to save Haku from dying. And she

---
[81] Yubaba has no taste, Zeniba complains. Needless to say, Zeniba lives much more modestly in her house in the woods. Zeniba is the 'at home' version of the workaholic Yubaba, as Miyazaki put it. Zeniba makes things, like Ursula in the forest in *Kiki's Delivery Service*: she knits and spins (and soon has No Face, the mouse and the insect working for her).

does. As Kamaji explains to Haku when he wakes, only love[82] can break the spell of Zeniba's golden seal,[83] and Zeniba confirms this to Chihiro back in the cottage.

In screenwriting terms, two-thirds in, before the climax begins, the heroine's given another task: to save Haku. This complicates the narrative (a common scripting device for a second act)), and is a thematic link to saving the parents (but is not directly linked). This's partly why Hayao Miyazaki says for him the movie's over during the train journey, because Chihiro has moved beyond selfish action and thought, and is putting others first.

There is no kiss for Chihiro and Haku,[84] but there is a sequence of ecstasy – and, in true form in a Hayao Miyazaki movie, the ecstasy of love is represented by flight. It occurs when Chihiro leaves Zeniba's cottage on Haku's back: the moment of love is also the moment of the breaking of the spell, when Chihiro remembers what happened to her as a child, when she fell into the River Kohaku to fetch her shoe. (The flashback, narrated by Chihiro, is seamlessly integrated into the film, as Chihiro and Haku fly at night above rivers and trees below).[85]

When Chihiro tells Haku his true name – Nigihayami Kohaku Nushi – the spell of naming is broken, and Haku returns to his boy form. As Chihiro and Haku plunge to earth together, they hold onto each other like skydivers, hand on hand. Chihiro is crying (but, in a detailed touch, her tears form around the top of her eyes, not the sides, because they are falling through the air). They press their heads together, the closest they come to kissing.

The ending of *Spirited Away* is very understated: no

---

[82] Kamaji uses the Japanese word *ai*, a strong term for their romance.
[83] The seal with the name on it plays into the theme of naming and magic in *Spirited Away*; seals also have a added meaning in Japan.
[84] They are framed in a medium close-up two-shot later, by the stream, the moment when in a conventional movie lovers would kiss. But this is *not* a conventional movie in any sense!
[85] The flashback is portrayed in a highly subjective, abstract fashion, very far away from the conventional form of filmmaking of long shots, establishing shots, and a sequence of images which have a traditional chronology.

action scene, and the transformation of Chihiro's parents back to human form takes place off-screen.[86] The lengthy *dénouement* of Chihiro catching up with her parents, reversing the journey at the start of the movie, isn't dramatically necessary: but it functions to allow the audience to leave the world of *Spirited Away* gently.

The Greek myth of Orpheus and Eurydice is evoked when Haku and Chihiro part: Haku can't cross the river to the human side of the abandoned theme park (recalling the folkloric belief that witches can't cross water). There is a boundary between the realm of the gods and that of humans, and a stream (which becomes an ocean) is as good a boundary line as any. (In *Howl's Moving Castle* the filmmakers place a similar flashback – into childhood – at a similar point in the narrative, and it's a flashback which brings the lovers closer to each other).

It's fitting that Haku should be the last character to be with Chihiro, as he was the first. Haku tells Chihiro to go and don't look back. And she doesn't. There's a moment when she nearly does, just before the tunnel, but then she remembers, and goes on, with her parents. Only in the final scene, reunited with her parents,[87] and on the far side of the tunnel, does Chihiro turn and look back down the tunnel.

And that is rightly a long moment, sustained on Chihiro in close-up, the culminating scene in the movie emotionally: because although an animated movie is only painted ink of plastic cels photographed and speeding through a projector at 24 frames a second, the audience can see that so much emotion is running through Chihiro, as she looks back at all

---

[86] For director Nobuhijo Obayashi, Chihiro's test at the end of *Spirited Away* was to show how much she loved her parents; it wasn't about pigs (in *Kinema Jumpo*, special *Spirited Away* issue, August 15, 2001).
[87] The touch of the car being covered with leaves and dusty inside, suggesting that many days have passed (or maybe weeks or even longer), is absolutely right. It's also spot-on that Chihiro's parents don't think any time has passed at all since they last saw Chihiro. Notice how the parents' transformation from pigs to humans takes place off-screen, and now it's the parents who're up ahead, calling to Chihiro to hurry up.

she has experienced, and all the characters she has known.[88]

The re-union between Chihiro and her folks is very understated. No hugs, no joyful tears; instead, her parents admonish her for taking so long, and Chihiro asks if they are all right. As far as they are concerned, nothing has happened. Chihiro is back to reality with a thump – and the movie suggests that it's going to be as difficult as it would have been before. Except now Chihiro has learned a few things, including one or two skills, which will help her in her life.

Spirited Away has transcended every limitation of technology and hardware and mechanisms to become a living, breathing thing. Critics said that no one would sit still for a full-length animated movie when Walt Disney produced his 'folly' in Hollywood in 1937 (*Snow White and the Seven Dwarfs*), and *Spirited Away* proves that, yes, they will, and an animated picture can be every bit as emotional and cathartic as a live-action movie.

---

[88] C. Odell and M. Le Blanc note that neither of Chihiro's parents have learnt anything from their experience – they have forgotten everything that happened to them (O, 118). But Chihiro hasn't forgotten. If Chihiro's parents' generation have let her down, the movie suggests that Chihiro will make up for it.

RESOURCES

WEBSITES

One of the best sources on the internet for Hayao Miyazaki information is nausicaa.net. Also the Studio Ghibli websites: onlineghibli.com, ghibli.jp and Ghibliworld.com. Anime News Network is excellent. There are fan sites, of course.

BOOKS

Among books in English, Helen McCarthy's book (1999, revised 2002) is essential reading. Dan Cavallaro's *The Animé Art of Hayao Miyazaki* is superb. Colin Odell and Michele Le Blanc's study of Studio Ghibli is useful, as is Andrew Osmond's study of *Spirited Away*.

AVAILABILITY

All of Hayao Miyazaki's films (and those of Studio Ghibli) are available for Western viewers on video and DVD (and, more recently, Blu-ray). They usually have the original Japanese language soundtrack, plus subtitles, and an English language dub.

The distributors of the movies of Hayao Miyazaki in Japan are: Toei Company. Tokuma Shoten. Toho.
In the U.S.A.: Buena Vista Home Video. Touchstone. Walt Disney Pictures. Miramax Films.

DIFFERENT VERSIONS

For Western viewers, the films of Hayao Miyazaki (and Studio Ghibli) are available in two main versions: the Japanese original version (usually with subtitles), and the dubbed versions.

Hayao Miyazaki's movies have been given very high profile English language dubs, by some of the best technical people in the business (sound mixes at Skywalker Sound, for instance), and high profile voice casts.

However, despite the laudable efforts of the Walt Disney Company, in terms of the quality of filmmaking, and the significance of Hayao Miyazaki as a filmmaker, the original language versions are always the ones to go for. Why? Because Miyazaki himself has overseen or approved of these voice casts and mixes (as well as the dialogue).

Think of it in the opposite direction: a film by Orson Welles or Alfred Hitchcock that was dubbed into Japanese, even by the best technical staff and the best actors in the Japanese film business, could not be regarded as conforming completely to the filmmakers' vision (unless Welles or Hitch could speak or understand Japanese and were present at the ADR and sound mixing and editing sessions).

It is also the case that Hayao Miyazaki is such a dynamically visual storyteller, dialogue, though important, is only one of numerous devices that Miyazaki and his teams employ. Unlike some movies, you really don't need to have the dialogue translated, via subtitles or dubbing, to know what's going on.

QUOTES BY HAYAO MIYAZAKI

I'm not going to make movies that tell children, 'You should despair and run away'.
•
Is someone different at age 18 or 60? I believe one stays the same.
•
I never read reviews. I'm not interested. But I value a lot the reactions of the spectators.
•
Don't watch animation! You're surrounded by enough virtual things already.
•
I'm not making a film; instead, it feels like the film is making me.
•
I am an animator. I feel like I'm the manager of an animation cinema factory. I am not an executive. I'm rather like a foreman, like the boss of a team of craftsmen. That is the spirit of how I work.
•
I'm really not good at depicting the bad guys, frankly. They always wind up to be people who are at the core basically good.
•
I can't do a film after having debated it. I am unable to do a film while discussing it with my team. I issue directives. I do not achieve it otherwise.
•
We live in an age when it is cheaper to buy the rights to movies than to make them.
•
If you watch something for three minutes, you feel like you know everything about it, even what went on backstage, and then you don't feel like watching the rest.
•
When a man is shooting a handgun, it's just like he is shooting because that's his job, and he has no other choice.

It's no good. When a girl is shooting a handgun, it's really something.

•

The 21st century is a complex and unforeseeable epoch. Our thinking habits and our values, which until now looked settled, are being challenged.

•

Personally I am very pessimistic. But when, for instance, one of my staff has a baby you can't help but bless them for a good future. Because I can't tell that child, 'Oh, you shouldn't have come into this life.' And yet I know the world is heading in a bad direction. So with those conflicting thoughts in mind, I think about what kind of films I should be making.

•

Modern life is so thin and shallow and fake. I look forward to when developers go bankrupt, Japan gets poorer and wild grasses take over.

CRITICS ON *SPIRITED AWAY*

Extracts from reviews of *Spirited Away*.

Miyazaki goes for – and gets – the big picture, the grand emotion, one spectacular set piece stacked on another in brilliant colors and design. There's not a more impressive sequence in recent movies than the arrival at the bathhouse of a huge, amorphous river-god, encased in centuries' worth of stink and sludge, whom Chihiro has the daunting task of giving a sturdy wash and scrub. It's a visual aria, whose suspense is topped only by the scene's surprise payoff. Artful but not arty, *Spirited Away* is a handcrafted cartoon, as personal as an Utamaro painting, yet its breadth and heart give it an appeal that should touch American viewers of all ages.
    Richard Corliss, *Time*
•
Spirited Away, which was even more popular in Japan than *Titanic*, is the most deeply and mysteriously satisfying animated feature to come along in ages... Miyazaki gives you almost too much to look at, yet it is never enough. The delicate wash of imagery in a sequence like the one in which a spectral train moves along tracks submerged in water gives way to colors as eye-poppingly sharp as M & Ms. Unlike even the best American animators – or just plain filmmakers, for that matter – Miyazaki doesn't gloss over the terrors of childhood, which here yield their own disquieting beauty. He respects the deep silences of his story, as well as its cacophonies. (The soundtrack is every bit as inventive as the visuals.) Very young children are apt to be frightened by this film, but older ones will recognize in Miyazaki, as with all great fabulists, a kindred spirit.
    Peter Rainer, *New York Magazine*
•
It would be a masterpiece in any language.
    Luke Y. Thompson, *Dallas Observer*
•
It's enchanting and delightful in its own way, and has a good heart. It is the best animated film of recent years, the latest work by Hayao Miyazaki, the Japanese master who is a god to the Disney animators.
    Roger Ebert, *Chicago Sun-Times*
•
It will disturb you as much as thrill you, make you wonder whether the boundaries between life and death, reality and fantasy, imagination and insanity are ever what they appear to be.
    Andrew O'Hehir, *Salon.com*
•
Turns everything we know about the contemporary world on its head, and substitutes it with one in which spirits, monsters, magicians and animals mix it

up in a carnival of energy, good humor and freewheeling illusion.
Jack Mathews, *New York Daily News*

•

A Japanese cross between *Alice in Wonderland* and *The Wizard of Oz* – is such a landmark in animation that labeling it a masterpiece almost seems inadequate.
Lou Lumenick, *New York Post*

•

Wondrously strange and just plain wonderful.
Steven Rea, *Philadelphia Inquirer*

•

A visual masterpiece about a scared little girl's breathtaking journey of self-discovery. All of the fun is getting there.
Michael Sragow, *Baltimore Sun*

•

Miyazaki is a genius, and this film is a masterpiece; go see it.
Shawn Levy, *Portland Oregonian*

•

A triumph of psychological depth and artistic brilliance offered as the magical adventures of one skinny little girl.
Lisa Schwarzbaum, *Entertainment Weekly*

•

It is plainly, though not simply, a masterpiece from an acknowledged master of contemporary animation, and a wonderfully welcoming work of art that's as funny and entertaining as it is brilliant, beautiful and deep.
Joe Morgenstern, *Wall Street Journal*

•

Offers a ride worth taking – an excursion through a fantastical pop universe that is pure, enchanting magic. Try it; you'll like it.
Rene Rodriguez, *Miami Herald*

•

Spirited dazzles and entertains like no other movie this year. It also comes to a satisfying conclusion and never once seems to take shortcuts. Miyazaki is one of world cinema's most wondrously gifted artists and storytellers.
David Hunter, *Hollywood Reporter*

•

Probably like nothing you've ever seen before. In a cool world, it would be guaranteed not only the Best Animated Feature Oscar, but Best Picture as well.
Luke Y. Thompson, *New Times* (L.A.)

•

A wonderful encore, marked by the painstaking attention to detail and artful balance between terror and joy that make Miyazaki's work unique.
Tasha Robinson, *The A.V. Club*

•

A very nutty fruitcake, *Spirited Away* is characterized by wonderfully detailed animation, packed with incident and populated by all manner of comic creatures.
J. Hoberman, *Village Voice*

FILMOGRAPHIES

A filmography of the chief theatrical movies directed by Hayao Miyazaki.

The Castle of Cagliostro (1979).
Monkey Punch/ Tokyo Movie Shinsha. 100m.
Japanese release: December 15, 1979. U.S.A. release: Sept, 1980/ April, 1991.

Nausicaä of the Valley of the Wind (1984).
Nibariki/ Tokuma Shoten/ Hakuhodo. 116m.
Japanese release: March 11, 1984. U.S.A. release: June, 1985.

Laputa: Castle In the Sky (1986).
Nibariki/ Tokuma Shoten. 124m.
Japanese release: August 2, 1986. U.S.A. release: July, 1987/ April 1, 1989.

My Neighbor Totoro (1988).
Nibariki/ Tokuma Shoten. 86m.
Japanese release: April 16, 1988. U.S.A. release: May 7, 1993.

Kiki's Delivery Service (1989).
Nibariki/ Tokuma Shoten. 102m.
Japanese release: July 29, 1989. U.S.A. release: May 23, 1998 (video).

Porco Rosso (1992).
Nibariki/ TNNG. 93m.
Japanese release: July 20, 1992. U.S.A. release: October 9, 2003.

Princess Mononoke (1997).
Nibariki/ TNDG/ Toho. 133m.
Japanese release: July 12, 1997. U.S.A. release: October 7, 1999.

Spirited Away (2001).
Toho. 125m.
Japanese release: July 20, 2001. U.S.A. release: September 20, 2002.

Howl's Moving Castle (2004).
Toho. 119m.
Japanese release: November 20, 2004. U.S.A. release: June 6, 2005.

Ponyo On the Cliff By the Sea (2008).
Toho. 101m.
Japanese release: July 19, 2008. U.S.A. release: June 6, 2009.

SPIRITED AWAY

Sen to Chihiro no Kamikakushi/ Spirited Away (2001).

Toho. 125m.

Japanese release: July 20, 2001.
U.S.A. release: September 20, 2002.

Written and Directed by Hayao Miyazaki.

CAST

Rumi Hîragi – Chihiro/ Sen
Miyu Irino – Haku –
Mari Natsuki – Yubaba/ Zeniba
Takashi Naitô – Chihiro no otôsan
Yasuko Sawaguchi – Chihiro no okâsan
Tatsuya Gashûin – Aogaeru, Assistant Manager
Ryûnosuke Kamiki – Bô
Yumi Tamai – Rin
Yô Ôizumi – Bandai-gaeru
Koba Hayashi – Kawa no Kami
Tsunehiko Kamijô – Chichiyaku
Takehiko Ono – Aniyaku
Bunta Sugawara – Kamajî
Noriko Kitou – Additional Voices
Shiro Saito – Additional Voices
Ken Yasuda – Additional Voices

ENGLISH VOICE CAST

Daveigh Chase – Chihiro
Suzanne Pleshette – Yubaba/ Zeniba
Jason Marsden – Haku
Susan Egan – Lin
David Ogden Stiers – Kamajii

Lauren Holly – Chihiro's Mother
Michael Chiklis – Chihiro's Father
John Ratzenberger – Assistant Manager
Tara Strong – Bô
Mickie McGowan – Additional Voices
Jack Angel – Additional Voices
Bob Bergen – No-Face/ Frog/ Additional Voices
Rodger Bumpass – Additional Voices
Jennifer Darling – Additional Voices
Paul Eiding – Additional Voices
Sherry Lynn – Additional Voices
Mona Marshall – Additional Voices
Candi Milo – Additional Voices
Colleen O'Shaughnessey – Additional Voices
Phil Proctor – Additional Voices
Jim Ward – Additional Voices

CREW

Produced by Donald W. Ernst – producer, Lori Korngiebel – associate producer, John Lasseter – executive producer, Toshio Suzuki – producer, Yasuyoshi Tokuma – executive producer
Original Music by Joe Hisaishi
Cinematography by Atsushi Okui
Film Editing by Takeshi Seyama
Production Design by Norobu Yoshida
Art Direction by Yôji Takeshige
Jeff Deckman – assistant production manager
Masayuki Miyagi – assistant director
Atsushi Takahashi – assistant director
Kô'hei Endô – color managment system
Yukie Nomura – color design assistant
Kazuko Yamada – color design assistant
Michiyo Yasuda – color designer
Toshiaki Abe – sound effects support
Atsushi Aikawa – DTS mastering
Petra Bach – adr supervisor
Gregg Barbanell – foley artist
Jessica Gallavan – adr editor
Suminobu Hamada – surround mixing
Kaz Hayashi – sound: dolby digital/ DTS stereo
Takeshi Imaizumi – sound mixer & recordist
Kazumi Inaki – sound production
Shuji Inoue – sound: dolby digital/DTS stereo
Michihiro Ito – sound effects
Tamaki Kojo – sound production

Rie Komiya – sound effects assistant
Mayuka Miyazawa – sound effects support
Eiko Morikawa – sound effects support
Daisuke Murakami – sound effects assistant
Kazuaki Narita – sound effects support
Toru Noguchi – sound effects
Terry Porter – sound re-recording mixer: U.S.
Tetsuya Satake – sound mixer & recordist
Robert L. Sephton – American sound supervisor
Tsukuru Takagi – sound mixer and sound recordist
Noriko Tsushi – DTS mastering
Ayako Ueda – sound effects support
Robert Bagley – telecine operator
Thomas Baker – CAPS scene planning
Masaru Karube – digital animator
Mitsunori Katâma – digital animator
Miki Sato – digital animator
Yoichi Senzui – digital animator
Yuji Tone – digital animator
Hiroki Yamada – digital animator
Mikio Mori – consultant: dolby film
Wataru Takahashi – digital camera and composite operator, and digital cinematographer
Atsushi Tamura – digital camera and composite operator
Junji Yubata – digital camera and composite operator
Shinichi Abe – inbetween animator
Akihiko Adachi – inbetween artist
Masashi Ando – animation director
Mi Kyoung An – inbetween animator: DR Digital
Myoung Hio An – digital ink and paint artist
Seiko Azuma – inbetween animator
Eun Soon Byeon – inbetween animator: DR Digital
Hye Soon Byeon – inbetween animator: DR Digital
Hyun Mi Cho – inbetween animator: DR Digital
Hee Eun Choi – inbetween animator: DR Digital
Soon Hwa Choi – digital ink and paint artist
Hanako Enomoto – inbetween animator
Ayako Fuji – inbetween artist
Emiko Fujii – inbetween animator
Kaori Fujii – animator
Hideto Fujiki – inbetween animator
Maya Fujimori – inbetween animator
Naoko Fujitani – inbetween animator
Naoya Furukawa – animator
Shôgo Furuya – key animator
Makiko Futaki – animator
Natsuko Goto – inbetween animator
Hideyoshi Hamatsu – animator

Hideki Hamazu – key animator
Sun Ki Ham – digital ink and paint artist
Keumi Han – digital ink and paint artist
Shinji Hashimoto – animator
Satoshi Hattori – inbetween animator
Soo Kyung Her – digital ink and paint artist
Kumi Hirai – inbetween animator
Rie Hirakawa – inbetween animator
Motonobu Hori – inbetween animator
Akira Hosogaya – inbetween artist
Young Mi Huh – inbetween animator
Hiroshi Iijima – digital ink and paint artist
Takeshi Imamura – animator
Masami Inomata – inbetween animator
Masayo Iseki – digital ink and paint artist
Hiroaki Ishii – digital ink and paint checker
Kunitoshi Ishii – inbetween animator
Kuniyuki Ishii – animator
Nobushige Ishita – inbetween animator
Yukari Ishita – inbetween animator
Keiko Itogawa – background artist
Nozomu Ito – inbetween animator
Yumiko Ito – inbetween animator
Yoshitake Iwakami – inbetween animator
Emiko Iwayanagi – inbetween animator
Cheo Ho Jang – inbetween animator: DR Digital
Hyeon Soo Joung – inbetween animator: DR Digital
Sung Hee Jung – inbetween animator: DR Digital
Hyun Ju Jun – inbetween animator: DR Digital
Megumi Kagawa – animator
Tsutomu Kaichi – inbetween animator
Shizue Kaneko – animator
Mioko Katano – inbetween animator
Byong Yor Kim – digital ink and paint artist
Eun Young Kim – inbetween animator: DR Digital
Shigeru Kimishima – key animator
Ji Eun Kim – inbetween animator: DR Digital
Jin Wook Kim – digital ink and paint artist
Jung-Hee Kim – inbetween animator: DR Digital
Mi Sun Kim – digital ink and paint artist
Mung Sook Kim – digital ink and paint artist
Myoung Sun Kim – digital ink and paint artist
Tae Jong Kim – digital ink and paint artist
Yumiko Kitajima – inbetween animator
Ogura Kobo – background artist
Komasa – inbetween artist
Daizen Komatsuda – inbetween animator
Junko Komatsuzaki – inbetween animator

Rie Kondou – inbetween animator
Ken'ichi Konishi – animator
Fumie Konno – inbetween animator
Kitaro Kosaka – animator
Misuzu Kurata – animator
Bok Kyoung Kwon – inbetween animator: DR Digital
Do Hee Lee – digital ink and paint artist
Eun Kyung Lee – digital ink and paint artist
Hye Sung Lee – inbetween animator: DR Digital
Mi Ok Lee – inbetween animator: DR Digital
Sue Shang Lee – inbetween animator: DR Digital
Daisuke Makino – inbetween animator
Kiyoko Makita – inbetween animator
Reiko Mano – inbetween animator
Yu Maruyama – inbetween animator
Tadahito Matsubayashi – inbetween animator
Mariko Matsuo – animator
Masaru Matsuse – animator
Atsuko Matsushita – inbetween artist
Satoshi Mikage – inbetween animator
Tomoko Miyata – inbetween animator
Yoshiyuki Momose – animator
Naomi Mori – digital ink and paint artist
Takashi Mori – inbetween animator
Kanako Moriya – digital ink and paint checker
Yasuto Murata – inbetween animator
Rie Nakagome – inbetween animator
Hiroaki Nakajima – inbetween animator
Yuki Nakajima – inbetween animator
Kazuki Nakamoto – inbetween animator
Katsutoshi Nakamura – animator
Yohei Nakano – inbetween animator
Hisashi Nakayama – animator
Mai Nakazato – inbetween animator
Kumi Nanjo – digital ink and paint artist
Akiko Nasu – digital ink and paint artist
Sumie Nishido – inbetween animator
Atsushi Nishigori – inbetween artist
Hiromi Nishikawa – inbetween animator
Minori Noguchi – inbetween animator
Fumiko Oda – digital ink and paint checker
Gosei Oda – inbetween animator
Norihito Ogawa – inbetween animator
Masahiro Ohashi – inbetween animator
Minoru Ohashi – animation checker
Shin'ya Ôhira – animator
Mayumi Ohmura – inbetween animator
Kumiko Ohta – inbetween animator

Kyoko Okabayashi – inbetween animator
Rie Okada – digital ink and paint artist
Chika Okubo – inbetween animator
Masashi Okumura – inbetween animator
Fumino Okura – digital ink and paint artist
Takeyoshi Omagari – inbetween animator
Aya Onishi – inbetween artist
Kazuyoshi Onoda – animator
Katsu Ōshiro – animator
Masaru Oshiro – animator
Norihiro Ōsugi – animator
Miho Otsuka – inbetween animator
Akihiro Oyama – digital ink and paint artist
Ji Hyun Park – inbetween animator: DR Digital
La Sung Park – digital ink and paint artist
So Hwa Park – inbetween animator: DR Digital
Suk-Hwa Park – inbetween animator: DR Digital
Young Suk Park – inbetween animator: DR Digital
Eun Me Pyun – inbetween animator: DR Digital
Shinobu Saeki – inbetween animator
Michiko Saito – digital ink and paint artist
Saho Saito – inbetween animator
Masaya Saitou – animation checker
Reiko Sakai – inbetween animator
Masako Sakano – inbetween animator
Chikako Sasagawa – inbetween animator
Masako Sato – inbetween animator
Akiko Seki – inbetween artist
Jin Hyuk Seo – inbetween animator: DR Digital
Kum Sook Seo – inbetween animator: DR Digital
Yuka Shibata – inbetween animator: DR Digital
Tomotaka Shibayama – digital ink and paint artist
Tsutomu Shibutani – inbetween animator
Akira Shigino – digital ink and paint artist
Ritsuko Shiina – inbetween animator
Ikuko Shimada – inbetween animator
Akiko Shimizu – digital ink and paint artist
Masako Shinohara – animator
Naoyoshi Shiotani – inbetween animator
Hyun Ju Song – inbetween animator: DR Digital
Jee Young Soung – inbetween animator: DR Digital
Ryozo Sugiyama – inbetween animator
Makiko Suzuki – key animator
Mariko Suzuki – animator
Kanako Takahashi – digital ink and paint artist
Naoko Takahashi – inbetween animator
Noboru Takano – animator
Nobuyuki Takeuchi – key animator

Noriyuki Takeuchi – animator
Atsushi Tamura – animator
Atsuko Tanaka – animator: Telecom Animation Film
Haruka Tanaka – inbetween animator
Yuichi Tanaka – animator
Kumiko Tanihira – inbetween animator
Hitomi Tateno – animation checker
Kumiko Terada – inbetween animator
Masako Terada – inbetween animator
Akiko Teshima – inbetween artist
Akiko Toba – inbetween artist
Yoyoi Toki – inbetween animator
Keiko Tomizawa – inbetween animator
Jinko Tsuji – inbetween animator
Koujirou Tsuraoka – inbetween animator
Kazuyuki Ueda – inbetween animator
Yumiko Ukai – digital ink and paint artist
Yukari Umebayashi – inbetween animator
Hideo Watanabe – inbetween animator
Alexandra Weihrauch – inbetween artist
Hisako Yaji – inbetween animator
Chikako Yamada – inbetween animator
Ken'ichi Yamada – animator
Satoko Yamada – inbetween animator
Shinichiro Yamada – inbetween animator
Tamami Yamada – key animator
Atsushi Yamagata – animator
Hirômi Yamakawa – animator
Eiji Yamamori – key animator
Hideshi Yamamori – animator
Rie Yamamoto – inbetween animator
Akihiko Yamashita – animator
Muneyuki Yamashita – inbetween animator
Shôjurô Yamauchi – animator
Yukari Yamaura – inbetween animator
Morihiko Yano – inbetween animator
Masafumi Yokota – inbetween animator
Yuki Yokoyama – digital ink and paint artist
Hiromasa Yonebayashi – animator
Mi Kyoung Yoon – inbetween animator: DR Digital
Hideaki Yoshio – animator
Hea Yeop Yun – digital ink and paint artist
Motohiro Hatanaka – casting coordinator
Jamie Thomason – voice casting: English version
David Wright – voice casting: English version
Keiko Yagi – casting coordinator
Naomi Yasu – casting coordinator
Chris DeLaGuardia – color timer

Katie Hooten – post-production coordinator
Rich Mackay – US version
Kyoko Mizuta – assistant editor
Mary Beth Smith – negative cutter
Mutsumi Takemiya – assistant editor
Megumi Uchida – assistant editor
Joe Hisaishi – conductor
Joe Hisaishi – musician: piano
Kazumi Inaki – music production
Youmi Kimura – composer: song "Itsumo nando-demo"
Tamaki Kojo – music production
Masayoshi Okawa – music engineer
Shinichi Tanaka – orchestra recordist
Joe Hisaishi – orchestrator
Kazunori Miyake – orchestrator
Jun Nagao – orchestrator
Stephen Alpert – overseas promotion
Nao Amisaki – overseas promotion
Shokichi Arai – coordinator
Koichi Asano – merchandising development
Leo Chu – vice president of production
Cindy Davis Hewitt – adaptation: English version
Nozomi Fukuda – advertising producer
Mieko Hara – advertising producer
Donald H. Hewitt – adaptation: English version
Linda Hoaglund – subtitler: English
Hiroi Hosokawa – advertising producer
Minami Ichikawa – advertising producer
Tomomi Imai – merchandising development
Rieko Izutsu – merchandising development
Yasushi Kanno – advertising producer
Yusuke Kikuchi – advertising producer
Michiyo Koyanagi – advertising producer
Haruyo Moriyoshi – overseas promotion
Minako Nagasawa – public relations
Ai Nakanishi – advertising producer
Junichi Nishioka – public relations
Atsuo Ogaki – advertising producer
Naoto Okamura – advertising producer
Hiroyuki Orihara – advertising producer
Mikiko Takeda – overseas promotion
Masaru Tsuchiya – advertising producer
Morikazu Wakizaka – advertising producer
Kirk Wise – dialogue director
Robert Bagley – special thanks
Matthew Jon Beck – special thanks

BIBLIOGRAPHY

HAYAO MIYAZAKI

"Interview With Hayao Miyazaki ", *A-Club*, 19, June, 1987
The Art of Kiki's Delivery Service, Tokuma, Tokyo, 1989
"Hayao Miyazaki Interview", *Comic Box*, Oct, 1989
"Money Can't Buy Creativity", *Pacific Friend*, 18, 9, Jan, 1991
"Now, After *Nausicäa* Has Finished", *YOM* special, June, 1994
Hayao Miyazaki's Daydream Note, Japan, 1997
Points of Departure, 1979-1996, Tokuma Shoten, Tokyo, 1997
"A Modest Proposal", *Manga Max*, 15, February, 2000
"The Purpose of the Film", *Spirited Away*, 2001
Nausicaä of the Valley of the Wind, VIZ Media, San Francisco, CA, 2004
Tenku no Shiro Rapyuta, Tokuma Shoten, Japan, 2004
Tonari no Totoro, Tokuma Shoten, Japan, 2004
Shuna no Tabi, Tokuma Shoten, Japan, 2008
Starting Point, 1979-1996, tr. B. Cary & F. Schodt, Viz Media, San Francisco, CA, 2009

OTHERS

G. Adams, ed. *The Cambridge Guide to Children's Books in English*, Cambridge University Press, Cambridge, 2003
S. Adilman. "*Spirited Away* Gets Extra Word", Animation Cafe, 2002
M. Ando. Interview, *Spirited Away*, 2001
The Art of Spirited Away, VIZ Media, 2002
B. Babington *Biblical Epic and Sacred Narrative in the Hollywood*, Manchester University Press, Manchester, 1993
R. Bator, ed. *Signposts to Criticism of Children's Literature*, American Library Association, Chicago, 1983
J. Beck, ed. *Animation Art*, Flame Tree Publishing, London, 2004
E. Bell *et al*, eds. *From Mouse to Mermaid: The Politics of Film, Gender and Culture*, Indiana University Press,

Bloomington, IN, 1995

A. Benciveni. *Miyazaki: Il Dio Dell Animé*, La Mani, Genoa, 2003

I. Bergman. *The Magic Lantern: An Autobiography*, London, 1988

J. Bittner. *Approaches To the Fiction of Ursula K. Le Guin*, UMI Research Press, Ann Arbor, MI, 1984

D. Bordwell & K. Thompson. *Film Art: An Introduction*, McGraw-Hill Publishing Company, New York, NY, 1979

—. *Narration in the Fiction Film*, Routledge, London, 1988

—. *The Way Hollywood Tells It*, University of California Press, Berkeley, CA, 2006

J. Bower, ed. *The Cinema of Japan and Korea*, Wallflower Press, London, 2004

P. Brophy, ed. *Kaboom! Explosive Animation From America and Japan*, Museum of Contemporary Art, Sydney, 1994

J. Brosnan. *Future Tense: The Cinema of Science Fiction*, St Martin's Press, New York, NY, 1978

—. *Primal Screen: A History of Science Fiction Film*, Orbit, London, 1991

S. Bukatman. *Terminal Identity: The Virtual Subject in Postmodern Science Fiction*, Duke University Press, Durham, NC, 1993

E. Byrne & M. McQuillan, eds. *Deconstructing Disney*, Pluto Press, London, 1999

H. Carpenter. *J.R.R. Tolkien: A Biography*, Allen & Unwin, London, 1977

—. & M. Prichard. *The Oxford Companion to Children's Literature*, Oxford University Press, Oxford, 1984/ 1999

D. Cavallaro. *The Animé Art of Hayao Miyazaki*, McFarland, Jefferson, NC, 2006

J. Clarke. *Animated Films*, Virgin, London, 2007

J. Clements & H. McCarthy. *The Animé Encyclopedia*, Stone Bridge Press, Berkeley, CA, 2001

J.C. Cooper: *Fairy Tales: Allegories of the Inner Life*, Aquarian Press, 1983

J. Donald, ed. *Fantasy and the Cinema*, British Film Institute, London, 1989

P. Drazen. *Animé Explosion*, Stone Bridge Press, Berkeley, CA, 2003

K. Eisner. "Kiki Delivers the Goods", *Variety*, July 17, 1998

M. Eisner with T. Schwartz. *Work in Progress*, Penguin, London, 1999

Mircea Eliade. *Patterns in Comparative Religion*, Sheed & Ward, 1958

—. *Shamanism: Archaic Techniques of Ecstasy*, Princeton University Press, Princeton, NJ, 1972

—. *A History of Religious Ideas*, I, Collins, London, 1979

—. *Ordeal by Labyrinth*, University of Chicago Press, Chicago, IL, 1984
—. *Symbolism, the Sacred and the Arts*, Crossroad, New York, NY, 1985
M. Eliot. *Walt Disney: Hollywood's Dark Prince: A Biography*, Andre Deutsch, London, 1994
M.-L. von Franz: *An Introduction to the Interpretation of Fairy Tales*, Spring Publications, New York, 1970
S. Fritz. "Miyazaki Came To America To Talk", Animation Cafe, 1999
L . Goldberg *et al*, eds. *Science Fiction Filmmaking in the 1980s*, McFarland, Jefferson, 1995
J. Goodwin, ed. *Perspectives On Akira Kurosawa*, G.K. Hall, Boston, MA, 1994
R. Grover. *The Disney Touch*, Business One Irwin, Homewood, Illinois, 1991
P. Hardy, ed. *The Aurum Encyclopedia of Science Fiction*, Aurum, London, 1991
V. Haviland, ed. *Children and Literature: Views and Reviews*, Scott, Foresman, Glenview, IL, 1973
P. Hunt: *An Introduction to Children's Literature*, Oxford University Press, 1994
—. ed. *Children's Literature: The Development of Criticism*, Routledge, 1990
J. Hunter. *Eros In Hell: Sex, Blood and Madness in Japanese Cinema*, Creation Books, London, 1998
S.S. Jones. *The Fairy Tale: The Magic Mirror of Imagination*, Twayne, New York, NY, 1995
B.F. Kawin. *How Movies Work*, Macmillan, New York, NY, 1987
U.C. Knoepflmacher. *Ventures Into Childhood: Victorians Fairy Tales and Femininity*, University of Chicago Press, Chicago, IL, 1998
A. Kuhn, ed. *Alien Zone: Cultural Theory and Contemporary Science Fiction*, Verso, London, 1990
—. ed. *Alien Zone 2*, Verso, London, 1999
C. Lanier. "Spirited Away To the Working World", mag.awn.com, 2002
T. Ledoux & D. Ranney. *The Complete Animé Guide*, Tiger Mountain Press, Washington, DC, 1997
U. Le Guin. *The Earthsea Trilogy*, Penguin, 1979
—. *Tehanu*, Penguin, 1992
—. *The Other Wind*, Orion, London, 2001
—. *Tales From Earthsea*, Orion, London, 2001
M. Lüthi: *Once Upon a Time: On the Nature of Fairy Tales*, Indiana University Press, Bloomington, 1976
—. *The Fairy Tale as Art Form and Portrait of Man*, tr. John Erickson, University of Indiana Press, Bloomington, 1985
A. Levi. *Samurai From Outer Space*, Open Court, Chicago, IL,

1996
L. Maltin. *Of Mice and Magic: A History of American Animated Cartoons*, New American Library, New York, NY, 1987
—. *The Disney Films*, 3rd ed., Hyperion, New York, NY, 1995
C. Manlove. *Modern Fantasy*, Cambridge University Press, Cambridge, 1975
—. *From Alice to Harry Potter: Children's Fantasy in England: Children's Fantasy in England*, Cybereditions Corporation, 2003
G. Mast *et al*, eds. *Film Theory and Criticism: Introductory Readings*, Oxford University Press, New York, NY, 1992a
—. & B Kawin, *A Short History of the Movies*, Macmillan, New York, NY, 1992b
H. McCarthy & J. Clements. *The Animé Movie Guide*, Titan Books, London, 1996
—. *The Erotic Animé Movie Guide*, Titan Books, London, 1998
—. "The House That Hayao Built", *Manga Max*, Apl 5, 1999
—. *Hayao Miyazaki: Master of Japanese Animation*, Stone Bridge Press, Berkeley, CA, 2002
A. Morton. *The Complete Directory to Science Fiction, Fantasy and Horror Television Series*, Other Worlds, 1997
S. Neale & M. Smith, eds. *Contemporary Hollywood Cinema*, Routledge, London, 1998
P. Nodelman: *Words About Pictures: The Narrative Art of Children's Picture Books*, University of Georgia Press, Athens, GA, 1988
C. Odell & M. Le Blanc. *Studio Ghibli: The Films of Hayao Miyazaki and Isao Takahata*, Kamera Books, London, 2009
I. & P. Opie: *The Classic Fairy Tales*, Paladin, 1980
T. Oshiguchi. "The Whimsy and Wonder of Hayao Miyazaki ', *Animerica*, 1, 5 & 6, July, 1993
A. Osmond. "*Nausicaä* and the Fantasy of Hayao Miyazaki", *SF Journal Foundation*, 73, Spring, 1998
—. "Hayao Miyazaki", *Cinescape*, 72, 1999
—. "Will the Real Joe Hisaishi Please Stand Up?", *Animation World Magazine*, 5.01, April, 2000
— *Spirited Away*, British Film Institute, London, 2003a
—. "Gods and Monsters", *Sight & Sound*, Sept, 2003b
D. Peary & G. Peary, eds. *The American Animated Cartoon*, Dutton, New York, NY, 1980
C. Platt. *Dreammakers: Science Fiction and Fantasy Writers At Work*, Xanadu, 1987
G. Poitras. *The Animé Companion*, Stone Bridge Press, Berkeley, CA, 1998
—. *Animé Essentials*, Stone Bridge Press, Berkeley, CA, 2001
M. Punch. *Lupin III*, vol. 13, Tokyopop, Los Angeles, CA, 2004
E. Rabkin & G. Slusser, eds. *Shadows of the Magic Lamp: Fantasy and Science Fiction in Film*, Southern Illinois

University Press, Carbondale, IL, 1985
T. Reider. *"Spirited Away"*, Film Criticism, 29, 3, Mch, 2005
D. Richie. *The Films of Akira Kurosawa*, University of California Press, Berkeley, CA, 1965
C. Rowthorn. *Japan*, Lonely Planet, 2007
K. Sandler. *Reading the Rabbit: Explorations in Warner Bros. Animation*, Rutgers University Press, Brunswick, NJ, 1998
R. Schickel. *The Disney Version: The Life, Times, Art, and Commerce of Walt Disney*, Pavilion, London, 1986
M. Schilling, "The Red Pig Flies To the Rescue", *Japan Times*, July 28, 1992
—. *Contemporary Japanese Film*, Weatherhill, New York, NY, 1999
—. "Majesty of 2-D", *Japan Times*, Nov 24, 2004
F. Schodt. *Dreamland Japan: Writings On Modern Manga*, Stone Bridge Press, Berkeley, CA, 1996
T. Shippey. *J.R.R. Tolkien: Author of the Century*, HarperCollins, London, 2000
G. Slusser. *The Farthest Shore of Ursula K. Le Guin*, Borgo Press, San Bernardino, CA, 1976
E. Smoodin. *Animating Culture: Hollywood Cartoons From the Sound Era*, Roundhouse, 1993
—. ed. *Disney Discourse: Producing the Magic Kingdom*, Routledge, London, 1994
V. Sobchack. *Screening Space: The American Science Fiction Film*, Ungar, New York, NY, 1987/1993
Spirited Away Roman Album, Tokuma Shoten, Tokyo, 2001
Rosemary Sutcliffe, *The Mark of the Horse Lord*, 1965
I. Takahata. "Interview", *Grave of the Fireflies*, DVD, 2004
—. "The Fireworks of Eros", in H. Miyazaki, 2009
M. Tatar. *The Hard Facts of the Grimms' Fairy Tales*, Princeton University Press, Princeton, NJ, 1987
—. *Off With Their Heads: Fairy Tales and the Culture of Childhood*, Princeton University Press, Princeton, NJ, 1992
J. Thomas: *Inside the Wolf's Belly: Aspects of the Fairy Tale*, Sheffield Academic Press, 1989
K. Thompson & D. Bordwell. *Film History: An Introduction*, McGraw-Hill, New York, NY, 1994
—. *Storytelling in the New Hollywood*, Harvard University Press, Cambridge, MA, 1999
J.R.R. Tolkien. *The Letters of J.R.R. Tolkien*, ed. H. Carpenter & C. Tolkien, Allen & Unwin, London, 1981
—. *The Monster and the Critics and Other Essays*, ed. C. Tolkien, Allen & Unwin, London, 1983
V. Watson, ed. *The Cambridge Guide To Children's Books in English*, Cambridge University Press, Cambridge, 2001
P. Wells. *Understanding Animation*, Routledge, London, 1998
J. Whalley & T.R. Chester: *A History of Children's Book*

Illumination, John Murray, 1988
C. Winstanley, ed. *SFX Collection: Animé Special*, Future Publishing, London
I. Wojcik-Andrews, ed. *The Lion and the Unicorn, Children's Films* issue, 20, 1, June, 1996
J. Zipes. *Breaking the Spell: Radical Theories of Folk and Fairy Tales*, Heinemann, London, 1978
—. *Fairy Tales and the Art of Subversion: The Classical Genre for Children and the Process of Civilization*, Heinemann, London, 1983
—. *Don't Bet on the Prince: Contemporary Feminist Fairy Tales in North America and England,* Methuen, New York, NY, 1986
—. *The Brothers Grimm: From Enchanted Forests to the Modern World*, Routledge, New York, NY, 1989
—. ed. *The Oxford Companion To Fairy Tales*, Oxford University Press, 2000
—. *Breaking the Spell: Radical Theories of Folk and Fairy Tales*, University of Kentucky Press, Lexington, 2002
—. *Sticks and Stones: The Troublesome Success of Children's Literature from Slovenly Peter to Harry Potter*, Routledge, London, 2002
—. *The Enchanted Screen: The Unknown History of Fairy-tale Films*, Routledge, New York, NY, 2011

JEREMY MARK ROBINSON has written many critical studies, including *Steven Spielberg: God-Light*, *Walerian Borowczyk*, *Arthur Rimbaud*, and *The Sacred Cinema of Andrei Tarkovsky*, plus literary monographs on: William Shakespeare; Samuel Beckett; Thomas Hardy; André Gide; Robert Graves; and John Cowper Powys.

It's amazing for me to see my work treated with such passion and respect. There is nothing resembling it in the U.S. in relation to my work.
Andrea Dworkin (on *Andrea Dworkin*)

This model monograph – it is an exemplary job, and I'm very proud that he has accorded me a couple of mentions... The subject matter of his book is beautifully organised and dead on beam.
Lawrence Durrell (on *The Light Eternal: A Study of J.M.W. Turner*)

His poetry is very good deep moving stuff.
Cloud Nine magazine

Jeremy Robinson's poetry is certainly jammed with ideas, and I find it very interesting for that reason. It's certainly a strong imprint of his personality.
Colin Wilson

Sex-Magic-Poetry-Cornwall is a very rich essay... It is a very good piece... vastly stimulating and insightful.
Peter Redgrove

ARTS, PAINTING, SCULPTURE

The Art of Andy Goldsworthy: Complete Works
Andy Goldsworthy: Touching Nature
Andy Goldsworthy in Close-Up
Andy Goldsworthy: Pocket Guide
Andy Goldsworthy In America
Land Art: A Complete Guide
Richard Long: The Art of Walking
The Art of Richard Long: Complete Works
Richard Long in Close-Up
Richard Long: Pocket Guide
Land Art In the UK
Land Art in Close-Up
Land Art In the U.S.A.
Land Art: Pocket Guide
Installation Art in Close-Up
Minimal Art and Artists In the 1960s and After
Colourfield Painting
Land Art DVD, TV documentary
Andy Goldsworthy DVD, TV documentary
The Erotic Object: Sexuality in Sculpture From Prehistory to the Present Day
Sex in Art: Pornography and Pleasure in Painting and Sculpture
Postwar Art
Sacred Gardens: The Garden in Myth, Religion and Art
Glorification: Religious Abstraction in Renaissance and 20th Century Art
Early Netherlandish Painting
Leonardo da Vinci
Piero della Francesca
Giovanni Bellini
Fra Angelico: Art and Religion in the Renaissance
Mark Rothko: The Art of Transcendence
Frank Stella: American Abstract Artist
Jasper Johns
Brice Marden
Alison Wilding: The Embrace of Sculpture
Vincent van Gogh: Visionary Landscapes
Eric Gill: Nuptials of God
Constantin Brancusi: Sculpting the Essence of Things
Max Beckmann
Gustave Moreau
Caravaggio
Egon Schiele: Sex and Death In Purple Stockings
Delizioso Fotografico Fervore: Works In Process 1
Sacro Cuore: Works In Process 2
The Light Eternal: J.M.W. Turner
The Madonna Glorified: Karen Arthurs

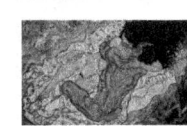

LITERATURE

J.R.R. Tolkien: The Books, The Films, The Whole Cultural Phenomenon
J.R.R. Tolkien: Pocket Guide
Beauties, Beasts and Enchantment: Classic French Fairy Tales
Tolkien's Heroic Quest
Sexing Hardy: Thomas Hardy and Feminism
Thomas Hardy's *Tess of the d'Urbervilles*
Thomas Hardy's *Jude the Obscure*
Thomas Hardy: The Tragic Novels
Love and Tragedy: Thomas Hardy
The Poetry of Landscape in Hardy
Wessex Revisited: Thomas Hardy and John Cowper Powys
Wolfgang Iser: Essays and Interviews
Petrarch, Dante and the Troubadours
Maurice Sendak and the Art of Children's Book Illustration
Andrea Dworkin
Cixous, Irigaray, Kristeva: The *Jouissance* of French Feminism
Julia Kristeva: Art, Love, Melancholy, Philosophy, Semiotics and Psychoanalysis
Hélene Cixous I Love You: The *Jouissance* of Writing
Luce Irigaray: Lips, Kissing, and the Politics of Sexual Difference
Peter Redgrove: Here Comes the Flood
Peter Redgrove: Sex-Magic-Poetry-Cornwall
Lawrence Durrell: Between Love and Death, East and West
Love, Culture & Poetry: Lawrence Durrell
Cavafy: Anatomy of a Soul
German Romantic Poetry: Goethe, Novalis, Heine, Hölderlin
Novalis: *Hymns To the Night*
Feminism and Shakespeare
Shakespeare: *The Sonnets*
Shakespeare: Love, Poetry & Magic
The Passion of D.H. Lawrence
D.H. Lawrence: Symbolic Landscapes
D.H. Lawrence: Infinite Sensual Violence
Rimbaud: Arthur Rimbaud and the Magic of Poetry
The Ecstasies of John Cowper Powys
Sensualism and Mythology: The Wessex Novels of John Cowper Powys
Amorous Life: John Cowper Powys and the Manifestation of Affectivity (H.W. Fawkn
Postmodern Powys: New Essays on John Cowper Powys (Joe Boulter)
Rethinking Powys: Critical Essays on John Cowper Powys
Paul Bowles & Bernardo Bertolucci
Rainer Maria Rilke
Joseph Conrad: *Heart of Darkness*
In the Dim Void: Samuel Beckett
Samuel Beckett Goes into the Silence
André Gide: Fiction and Fervour
Jackie Collins and the Blockbuster Novel
Blinded By Her Light: The Love-Poetry of Robert Graves
The Passion of Colours: Travels In Mediterranean Lands
Poetic Forms

POETRY

Ursula Le Guin: *Walking In Cornwall*
Peter Redgrove: Here Comes The Flood
Peter Redgrove: Sex-Magic-Poetry-Cornwall
Dante: Selections From the *Vita Nuova*
Petrarch, Dante and the Troubadours
William Shakespeare: *The Sonnets*
William Shakespeare: Complete Poems
Blinded By Her Light: The Love-Poetry of Robert Graves
Emily Dickinson: Selected Poems
Emily Brontë: Poems
Thomas Hardy: Selected Poems
Percy Bysshe Shelley: Poems
John Keats: Selected Poems
D.H. Lawrence: Selected Poems
Edmund Spenser: Poems
Edmund Spenser: *Amoretti*
John Donne: Poems
Henry Vaughan: Poems
Sir Thomas Wyatt: Poems
Robert Herrick: Selected Poems
Rilke: Space, Essence and Angels in the Poetry of Rainer Maria Rilke
Rainer Maria Rilke: Selected Poems
Friedrich Hölderlin: Selected Poems
Arseny Tarkovsky: Selected Poems
Paul Verlaine: Selected Poems
Novalis: *Hymns To the Night*
Arthur Rimbaud: Selected Poems
Arthur Rimbaud: *A Season in Hell*
Arthur Rimbaud and the Magic of Poetry
D.J. Enright: By-Blows
Jeremy Reed: *Brigitte's Blue Heart*
Jeremy Reed: *Claudia Schiffer's Red Shoes*
Gorgeous Little Orpheus
Radiance: New Poems
Crescent Moon Book of Nature Poetry
Crescent Moon Book of Love Poetry
Crescent Moon Book of Mystical Poetry
Crescent Moon Book of Elizabethan Love Poetry
Crescent Moon Book of Metaphysical Poetry
Crescent Moon Book of Romantic Poetry
Pagan America: New American Poetry

MEDIA, CINEMA, FEMINISM and CULTURAL STUDIES

J.R.R. Tolkien: The Books, The Films, The Whole Cultural Phenomenon
J.R.R. Tolkien: Pocket Guide
The *Lord of the Rings* Movies: Pocket Guide
The Ghost Dance: The Origins of Religion
Cixous, Irigaray, Kristeva: The *Jouissance* of French Feminism
Julia Kristeva: Art, Love, Melancholy, Philosophy, Semiotics and Psychoanalysis
Luce Irigaray: Lips, Kissing, and the Politics of Sexual Difference
Hélene Cixous I Love You: The *Jouissance* of Writing
Andrea Dworkin
'Cosmo Woman': The World of Women's Magazines
Women in Pop Music
Discovering the Goddess (Geoffrey Ashe)
The Poetry of Cinema
The Sacred Cinema of Andrei Tarkovsky
Andrei Tarkovsky: Pocket Guide
Andrei Tarkovsky: *Mirror*: Pocket Movie Guide
Andrei Tarkovsky: *The Sacrifice*: Pocket Movie Guide
Walerian Borowczyk: Cinema of Erotic Dreams
Jean-Luc Godard: The Passion of Cinema
Jean-Luc Godard: Pocket Guide
John Hughes and Eighties Cinema
Ferris Buller's Day Off: Pocket Movie Guide
The Cinema of Richard Linklater
Liv Tyler: Star In Ascendance
Blade Runner and the Films of Philip K. Dick
Paul Bowles and Bernardo Bertolucci
Media Hell: Radio, TV and the Press
An Open Letter to the BBC
Detonation Britain: Nuclear War in the UK
Feminism and Shakespeare
Wild Zones: Pornography, Art and Feminism
Sex in Art: Pornography and Pleasure in Painting and Sculpture
Sexing Hardy: Thomas Hardy and Feminism

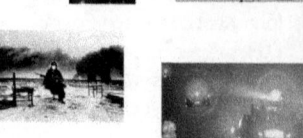

In my view *The Light Eternal* is among the very best of all the material I read on Turner.
(Douglas Graham, director of the Turner Museum, Denver, Colorado)

The Light Eternal is a model monograph, an exemplary job. The subject matter of the book is beautifully organised and dead on beam. (Lawrence Durrell)

It is amazing for me to see my work treated with such passion and respect. (Andrea Dworkin)

Sex-Magic-Poetry-Cornwall is a very rich essay... It is like a brightly-lighted box. (Peter Redgrove)

CRESCENT MOON PUBLISHING P.O. Box 393, Maidstone, Kent, ME14 5XU, England
0044-1622-729593 cresmopub@yahoo.co.uk www.crescentmoon.org.uk